A Character Studies

Vignettes in Words and Image

Scaramouche Black

Writing Knights Press — Cleveland, OH

A Character Studies
Writing Knights Press — Cleveland, Ohio

http://writingknights.com
http://facebook.com/writingknights

ISBN 978-1-97828-424-1

Copyright © 2017 Scaramouche Black

All Rights Reserved. No part of this publication may be reproduced, stored in a retrieval system, or transmitted, in any form or in any means – by electronic, mechanical, photocopying, recording or otherwise – without prior written permission.

These assorted ramblings and doodlings are devoted to a life interestingly-, if not always well-, lived in the Land of Cleve, with assorted diversions in more exotic locales.

They are dedicated to those who've stood by me through the proverbial thick and thin through sanity and in-. Deb, Az, Sky, Eric, Zoe, Dan, Cat, Ash, Todd, Jackie, Mae, Zia, Courage, Mattie, Lizzie, T, Emi, Kim, Tom, Tim, Adrienne, Laura, Vi, John, Jenny, Steve, Summer, Julie, Jen, Rob, Ron, Will, Vanessa, Rachel, Chris, Tony, Kayleigh, Gem, Ari, Lui, Vicky, Amanda, Kirsten...
All of you are beautiful and brilliant.
May your glimmer never fade.

Finally, I'd like to dedicate this book
to the illustrious and irreplaceable
Mr. Ross Martyn Hayes,
and to the beginning of a new life in the UK.

And finally, the most important dedication of all:
to LOVE, everlasting and unconquerable.

Without further ado, enjoy "A Character Studies"!

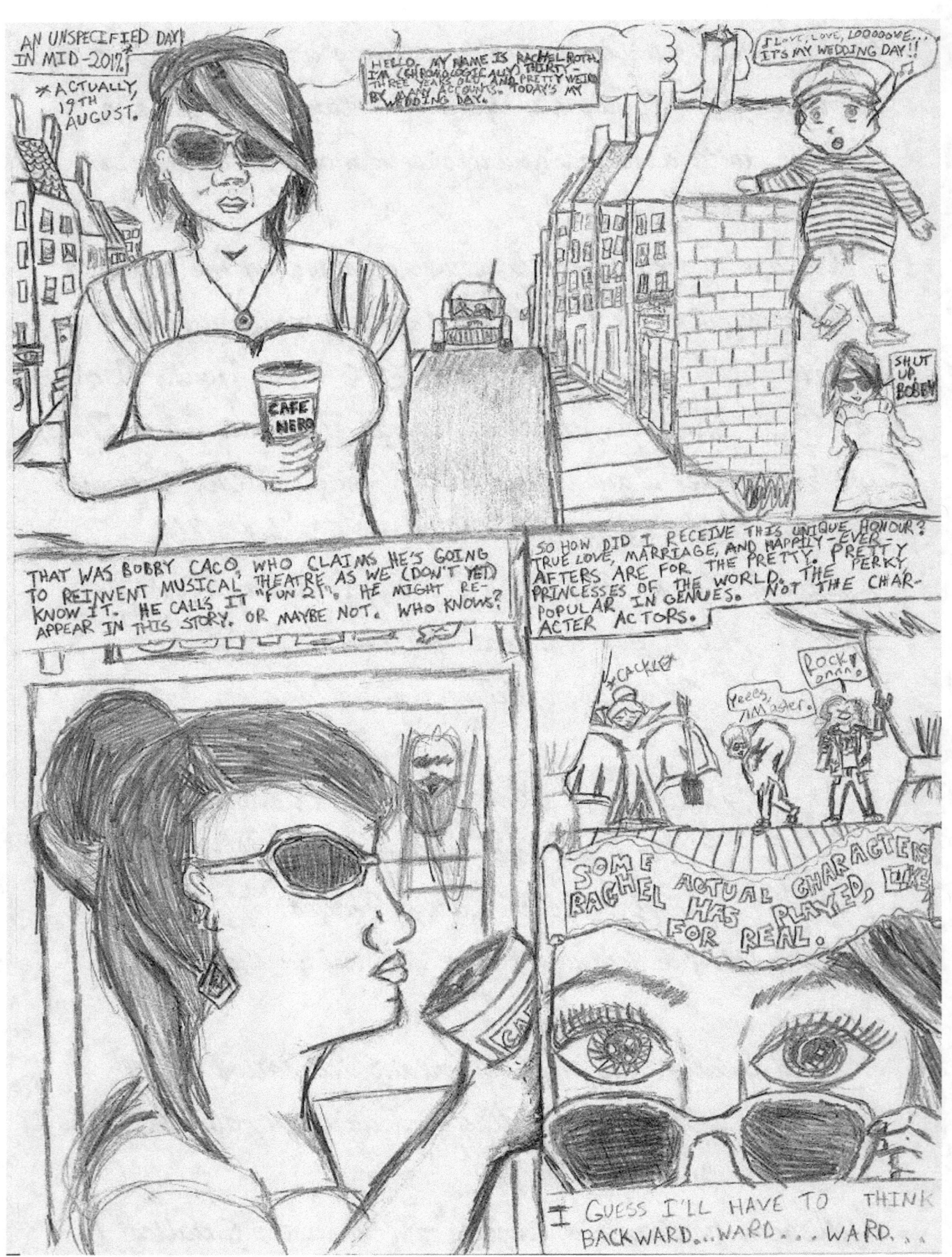

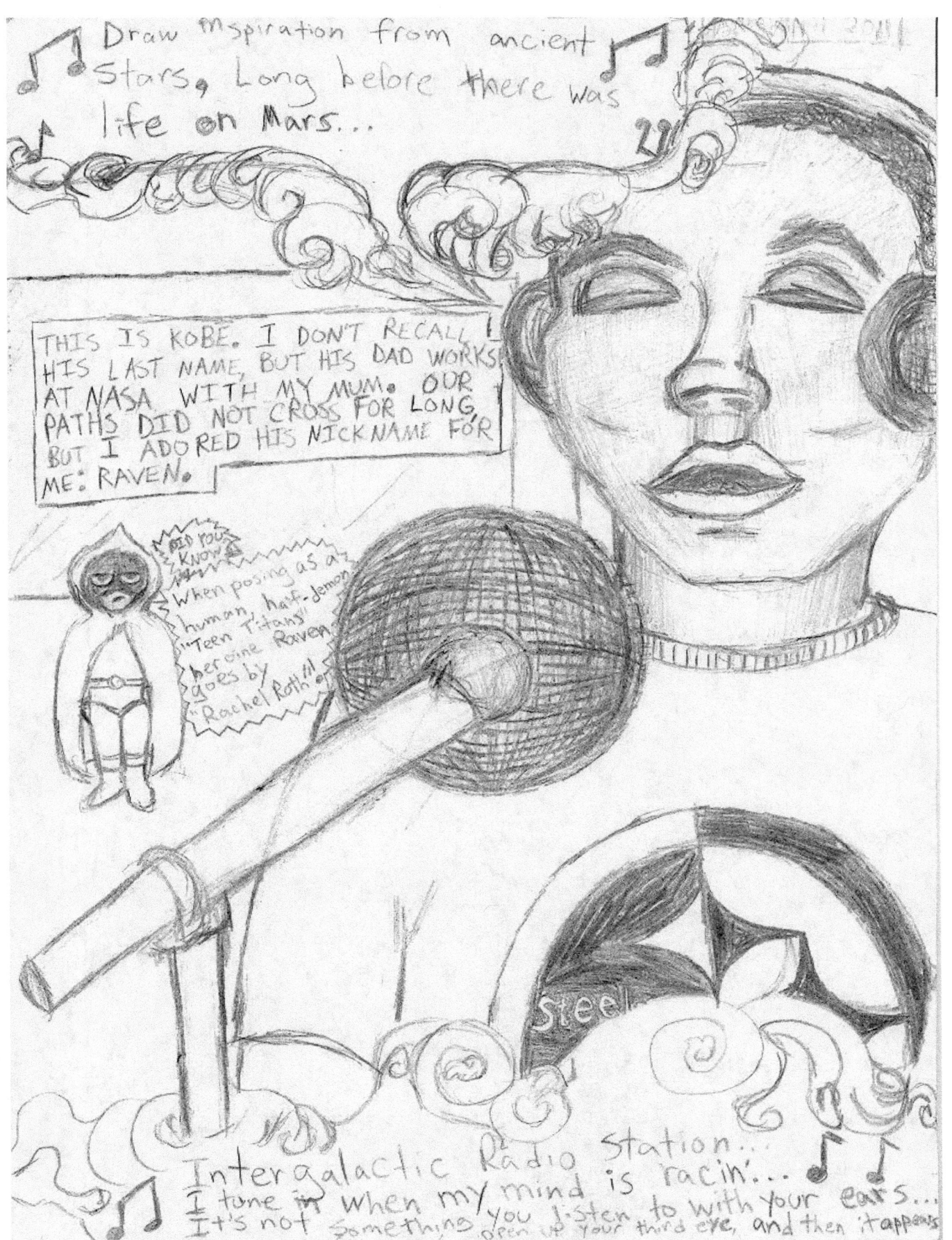

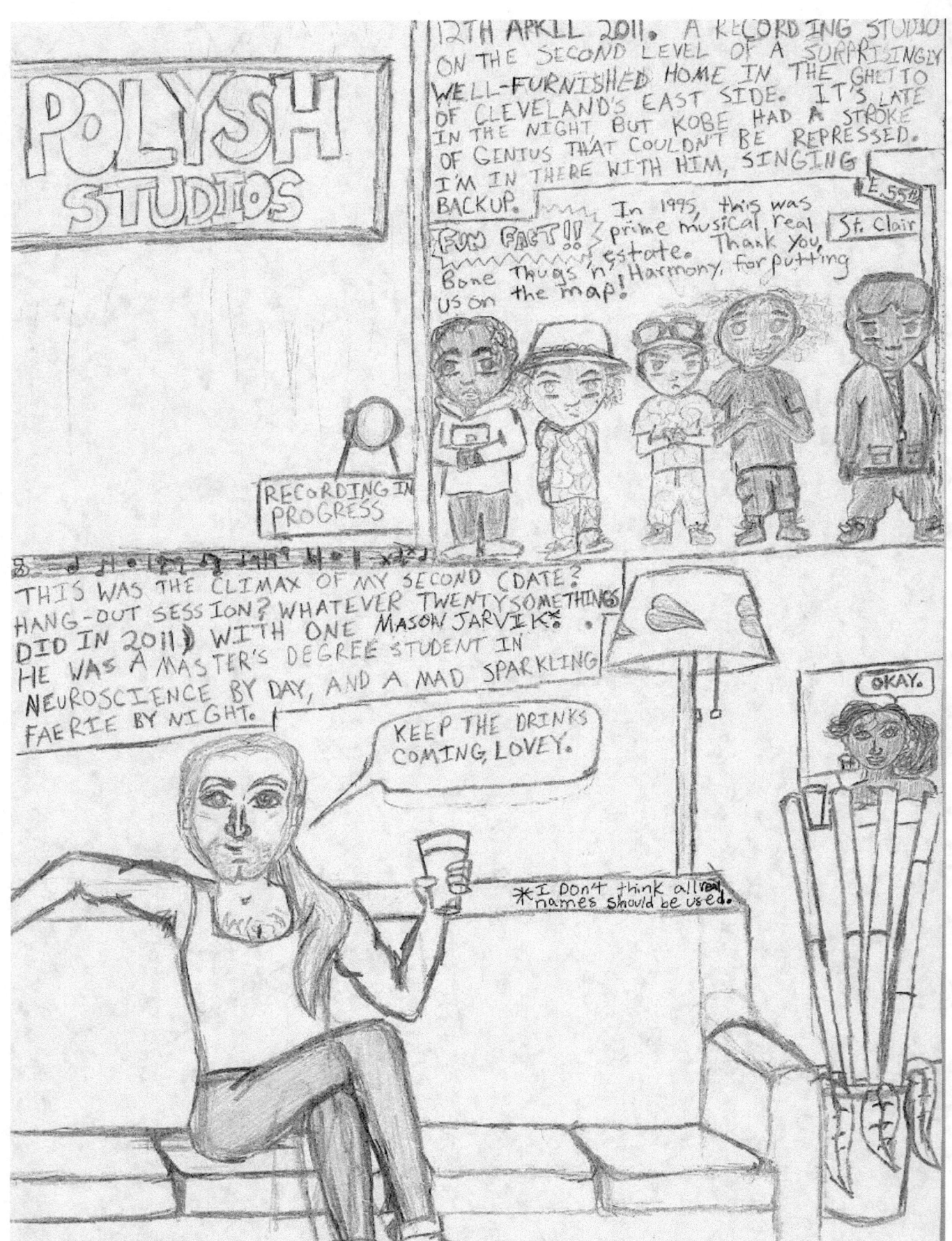

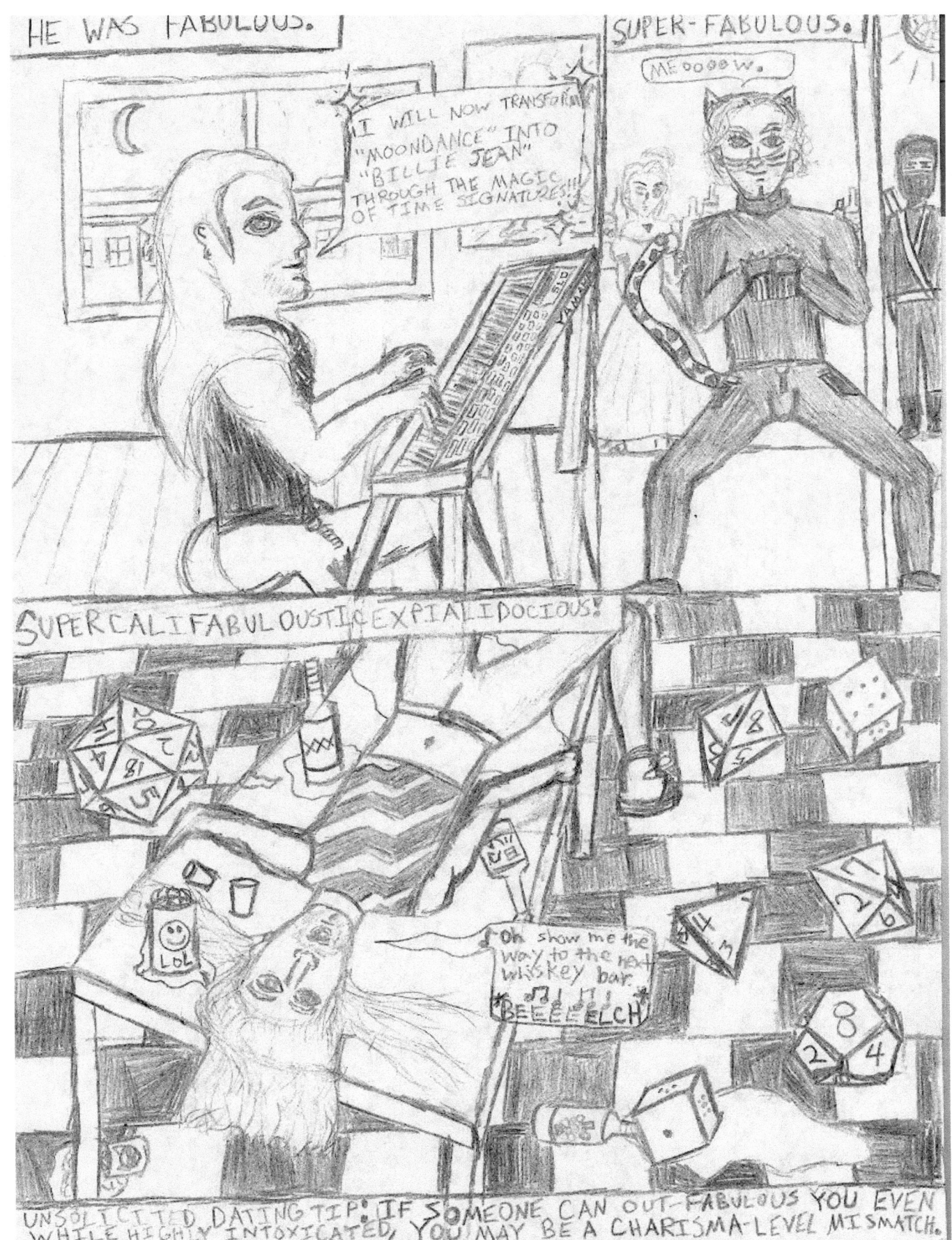

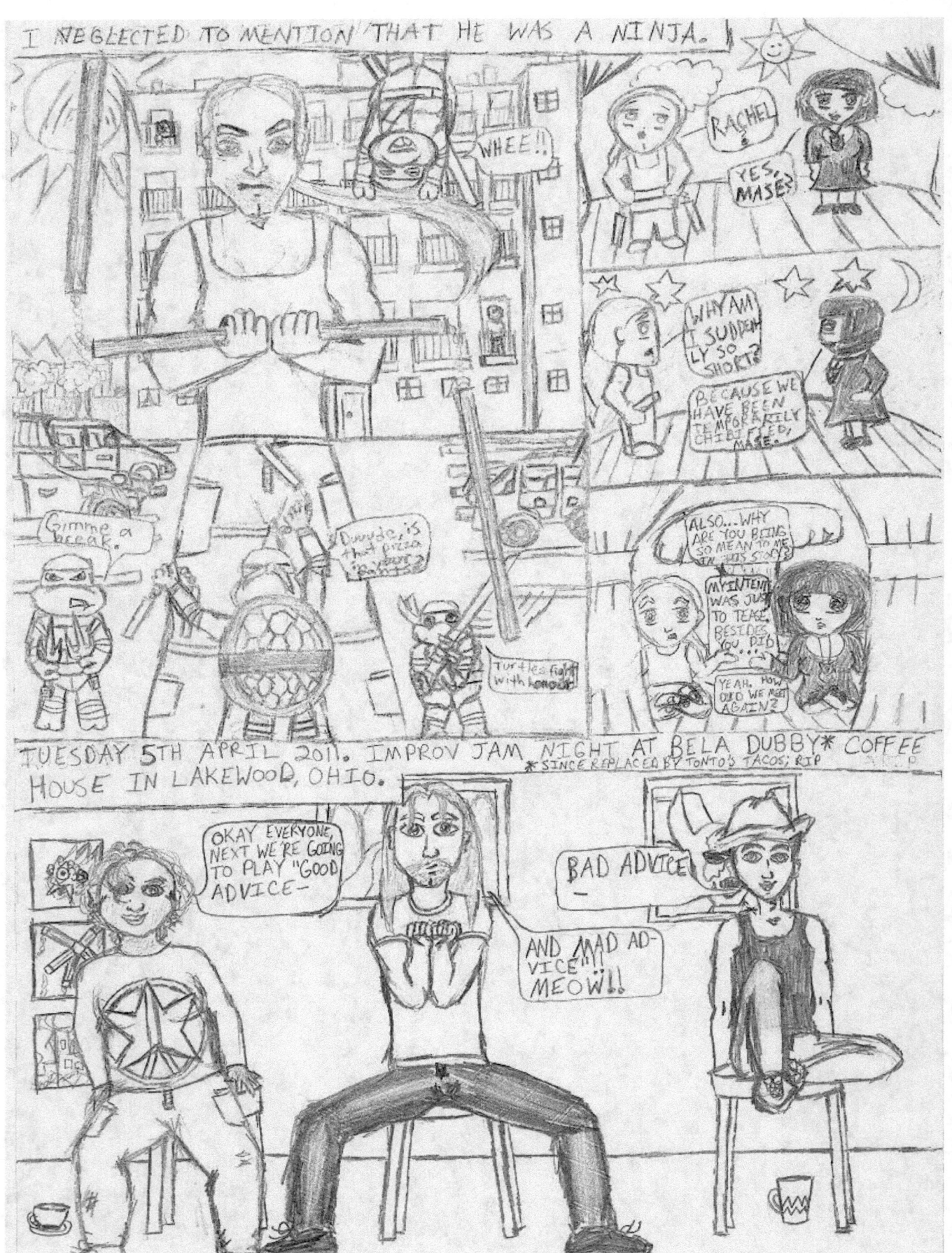

Con-templations

My first target was what the mainstream of society might politely refer to as a "BBW". While her girth and disharmonious facial features might render her invisible to men with goals different to my own, those traits drew me like a moth to the proverbial flame. Regarding her from across the University Student Centre's barroom, I knew I had to have her. Not just in a sexual sense, oh no. Hogging was a hobby for the younger students; undergrads perhaps. As a PhD candidate, I needed to set my sights a few degrees higher, and prioritise long-term security over immediate physical release. I was a grown-up now, and it was time I aimed to live like one.

The woman in question was one I vaguely recognised as a TA from the uni's English department. I wasn't certain of her specialty, but something about her appearance spoke of Medieval European mythos. I'd come across many like her in my twenty-seven years; bespectacled with frizzy, unkempt hair and clothing seemingly pilfered from a fortune teller's caravan. Being bullied in childhood often led such types to seek refuge in the works of fantasy which would later secure them careers in academia. It seemed likely we would find common ground.

My target looked up from the pile of essays she was marking, and sipped her pint. She was a beer girl, which boded well. There would be no delusions of worth to contend with; no pretension. She knew how the world viewed her, and she was through trying to contest it. I met her gaze and flashed her a disarming half-smile. She immediately looked down and returned to her marks. I thought a slight blush touched her cheeks, but couldn't be sure. It was time to escalate.

I made my way over and introduced myself. She responded in kind, citing her name as Helen (ironic), and commenting that she'd seen me about campus. She seemed impressed by my area of study (particle physics), and offered to buy me a drink. This was a lady who had resigned herself to filling the role of provider. Just what I was looking for. As the evening wore on and our alcohol levels rose, I wondered if there were any other possibilities to which this Helen might be open.

As it turned out there were quite a few. Five years later found us residing on the thirtieth floor of an elegant high-rise on English Sound. Our small yacht, the *Whitebeard Wizard,* was docked nearby. One fourth of the population of Vancouver owned watercraft, after all, and we had to keep up with the Joneses. I'd taken to the road for the first time in my life, and was the proud owner of a Nissan Maxima. My doctoral dissertation was still in progress, but I felt less rushed about the whole situation. After all, Helen had a cushy job (in the exact field I'd first presumed), and took good care of me.

Until she decided I wasn't worth it. One afternoon, as I sat slaughtering Nazis with my online buddies, she burst through the front door. An aura of rage buzzed about her head like the buildup to a lightning storm.

"Hon," she spoke, tainted treacle through a sewer grate of teeth, "We need to talk."

"Just a minute," I requested, latching onto my latest onscreen victim. "I'm killing Nazis."

Making full use of her elephantine heft, she lurched toward me and ripped the console from my hands. "No. Now."

"But this game is live, and I'll miss my chance at medals for myself and my troop!"

"Fuck you, DEAR." With a venomous smile, she used her free hand to unplug my beautiful new Xbox.

Anger is not an emotion which comes to me easily, but with that action, my wife of three years triggered it. I stood up, meeting her gaze and matching her inch for inch. I didn't want to fight, but I'd learned how to put her in her place when necessary. Flashing a shit-eating grin that might ALMOST have been mistaken for "kind" and crossing my arms, I nodded.

"What is THIS?"

It was then I noticed the stack of printouts she clutched in one hand. They'd looked like student papers at first, which were a common enough sight. She held them up for my perusal, revealing a bevy of nubile nudes in inviting positions. Apparently, she'd found transcripts of my Yahoo! Chat correspondences. I inhaled deeply – now was NOT the time to lose my cool.

"Porn, darling. You can't honestly expect to fulfill all my masculine urges on your own, can you?"

"Don't give me that. I've chatted with a few of these young ladies – Madison and Sam: twins, barely 18. Aren't you a little old to be playing in the sandbox?"

"Well, bully for you. You caught me conversing with a couple of girls online. I'm hardly the only one to do it."

"You're also a married man – and to be frank, you haven't brought much to the table in this relationship."

"I've given you my hand and my company. What more do you want?"

"Well, let's see. To begin with," there was a pregnant pause, as if she were debating whether to charge head-on into battle, "I'd like you to contribute."

"I cook. I clean." I prepared to argue my case, but Helen was not in a listening mood.

"You need to contribute financially. Find a job. An actual, paid position – not a get-rich-quick pyramid scheme or a paid gaming "opportunity"."

"Gaming is the only thing which brings me joy!"

With that comment, whatever string of sanity had tethered my wife to Earth, reining her in, snapped. A bestial growl issued from somewhere in her porcine belly, and she ground her hoof against the floor like a bull ready to face its matador. A passing familiarity with Spain's national sport told me the odds were in my favour. I'd come through this.

Regaining an ounce of composure as well as her voice, Helen countered. "Obviously, not the only thing. You seem to relish online chats with little girls."

"Now, now dear," I smirked, "You and I both know feminine beauty peaks in the late teens or early twenties. Can you really fault me for looking?"

"No..., but I CAN fault you for engaging in explicit conversations, constructing elaborate BDSM roleplay scenarios, and making arrangements to use our house as a playground while I continue to work so you can live as a man of leisure in one of the world's most expensive cities." Though she had calmed considerably, her voice grew louder as she plodded toward me, sorting through the paper stack in her hand until she found what she was seeking.

"And do you know what, DEAREST? This time I AM going to fault you. I've made one attempt after another to rationalise your behaviour to my friends and parents. 'Oh, he's busy with his studies,' I've said. 'When he's finished his dissertation, he'll have no trouble finding a great job, and then it will be *his* turn to provide for *me*.' But we've been married for three years, and if I'm not mistaken you've been working on your PhD for seven. But how long has it been since you've actually gotten any work done on your dissertation? I haven't seen you on campus at all for at least a term, and from what I've seen, you're more invested in Call of Duty, Halo, and sexploits than you are in particle physics."

Although I could feel a slow rage simmering within me, I kept it from boiling over. "What are you suggesting? It's true that I'm taking a break right now. Would you rather I burn out on particle physics, and never finish my PhD at all? Would you rather I flip burgers at McDonald's, perhaps, or take a job at a sweatshop in International District?"

The woman who'd offended my eyes in just the right way all those years ago heaved a sigh and fell heavily into the plush seat where I'd sat moments before, happily striving toward battlefield victory. She'd never struck me as vivacious or youthful but now, at 36 years of age, she reminded me of living death. "You know, a short while ago I might have said yes. But that's not what I want. I want you to detach your loathsome, leeching self from my life as soon as you can. Tomorrow, I'm filing for divorce." She punctuated her point by thumping her pile of "evidence".

I reached as quickly as I could manage toward Helen's stack of papers, but she'd anticipated the maneuver. Her closest foot jutted out, and before I know what had happened I was lying supine between her chair and our 52" flat-screen TV; my legs on the floor and the upper half of my back atop a now-shattered coffee table. I screamed. Though adrenaline pulsed through my veins, it did not numb my dislocated shoulder, nor did it keep me from feeling each tiny shard of glass which now pierced my skin.

"You fat, pre-menopausal hog! I'm going to sue you for everything you're worth!"

I attempted to do so. While Canada's National Health Care did not let me down, I was in just sorry enough shape for just long enough to garner a fair bit of sympathy in court. I made out quite nicely – the condo, most of the furniture, the Nissan, two laptops and a state-of-the-art gaming PC, and the Xbox all came into my possession. For the moment, I had everything required for a comfortable existence.

***

It's said that men crave freedom; that we detest being "tied down" and will do all we can to avoid it. While I'd never been frightened of commitment per se, there was something beautiful and ecstatic about having the house to myself; about waking in the morning and feeling free to eat whatever I wished – or not eat at all. I was free to read or speak with whomever I'd like online or in person. On any given day I could head out to my local CakeMakers chapter, or attend a Young Professionals' networking event, without the fear of being tracked by a jealous harpy. I could watch football without being shot death stares and tutted at.

The clarity that came with my newfound freedom encouraged me to manage time more effectively, and within a year I'd earned my PhD. As a doctor (I saw no reason to tell them what sort) with a home in the posh part of town, I found the young beauties flocked to me. I had quite a harem at one point – Chinese, Greek, Mexican, Polish, and Nigerian, along with a plain-ish, geeky redhead who'd learn her place once the glow of youth left her in the lurch. Of course, I was not able to extract anything of lasting value from my feminine visitors. They were students and party girls without much to offer apart from their flesh. But there was plenty to enjoy on that count.

I was broke, of course, but what my bedroom companions didn't know couldn't hurt them. They saw my shiny degree and shinier condo, and assumed they had found themselves a sugar daddy. Some I'd string along for a while, tempting them with cheap liquor and talk of my research which flew far over their heads. Others I'd tell the truth, leaving them to take a thirty story "elevator ride of shame", after the fact.

Things were going alright, but after eighteen months the last of my court winnings had dwindled to practically nothing, and my bills were not going to pay themselves. While the condo was paid in full, residing in a well-furnished box without electricity or heat wouldn't do at all. It was time to find a new benefactor.

* * *

CakeMakers is one of the few non-virtual social activities in which I take pleasure. If you haven't heard of the organisation, I feel mildly sorry for you. Founded in 1922, it's a public speaking group which helps people hone their communication and leadership skills. If it weren't for CakeMakers, I would never have gotten through my socially awkward adolescent phase, and would most likely still be a virginal basement dweller without a BA, let alone a PhD.

While I find most people terribly uninteresting and stupid, CakeMakers has been of assistance in dealing with the average Joe or Jane's inane prattle, and appearing to actually listen. In general, one garners a more favourable response when people feel that person cares about their trivial concerns. Do others truthfully take interest in the day-to-day affairs of their fellow man, or is it always as much of a farce as I find it? Perhaps it's a matter of needing to study what comes instinctively to most.

Usually the organisation's local chapters (one sober and family-friendly, the other decidedly not) are enough to keep me engaged and entertained. However, when the financial and temporal means are available, their weekend seminars and biannual conventions can be immensely fun. Studying ordinary humans and their communications, in addition to practicing the arts of debate, drunken alliance formation, and Game, are worthwhile ways to spend three or four days.

In 2009, eight years after my first divorce, I was lucky enough to engage in a tryst with a wealthy, but exceptionally plain, lady from the online gaming community. At first she gave into my every demand, making my pleasure her sole goal and paying my bills like a good little warted toadie, but then her romance was rekindled with her husband, and the charming man who'd seen her through months of isolation was no longer a priority. As my utilities were shut off, I began to panic – but a bit of blackmail earned me a few more months of security, and left me with just enough extra to secure myself a ticket for the August 2010 CakeMakers convention in Carson City, Nevada.

This convention would present the perfect opportunity to put my skills as a CakeMaker to the test. I would enter the hotel as a highly-educated pauper, but I would leave with a wealthy career woman, and perhaps her ring, wrapped around my finger. If the cards were played correctly, I would never again want for anything.

My first few days at the Carson City Hilton were uneventful. I went to a panel exploring better delivery techniques for Coffee Table Topics (the bread and butter of most run-of-the-mill meetings) hosted by a butch lady named Julie Ramirez, and another on "cold-reading" techniques hosted by celebrity medium Joe Mason. Regrettably, Mr. Mason didn't have too much new to teach me. In fact, throughout most of both those workshops my mind began to wander, and I found myself putting such tactics to use.

It was interesting to note the crowds that were drawn to given topics and hosts. Ms. Ramirez, for instance, drew a crowd of 80% androgynous fat-arsed tattooed and pierced bikers with a disregard for personal hygiene. Most were probably women, but it's hard to be certain with bull-dykes. I noted a few women on the younger end of things, relatively speaking (we must speak in relative terms since the average age of women in CakeMakers is about 65) who were at least identifiable as such. One had spiky blue hair and a pierced septum, while the other sported long magenta locks. They were probably feminists, which my experience had shown me meant they could probably be easily bedded and convinced to at least feign enjoying the act. I considered approaching, but in the end refrained. In modern gynocentric culture, even fours often felt entitled to dates.

Joe Mason's workshop gave me the disconcerting impression that I had been cloned as part of a government project, and was only now being granted access to the truth about my existence. Or that I was somehow positioned in the most convincing "hall of mirrors" funhouse illusion ever conceived. Phenotypically, there was a high degree of similarity among the talk's attendees. Many of us sported glasses that told tales of imperfect vision rather than hipsterdom, and most were either near the point of morbid obesity or seemingly malnourished, and the adenoidal grumblings and hacks which echoed throughout the meeting room told me was not alone in suffering allergies. I wondered if the other attendees at this panel were also interested in "reading people" so as to nudge the workings of the universe, so heavily biased against the physically imperfect, slightly more in our direction. We were not an attractive bunch – yet we were men, which was one thing in our favour.

The cold-reading workshop went on way too long; artificially extended by a frumpy witch who insisted the man contact a procession of her deceased pets. Apparently it hadn't occurred to her that with this workshop, the famed "medium" was basically declaring himself a fraud. Yet, after Fluffy and Prudence and Agent Bowwow had put in their respective appearances and the panel finished at long last, I took note of the middle-aged lady who'd requested the metaphysical display. Especially once I noticed her Prada suit. The garment's fine tailoring indicated it was the genuine article, which signaled that she was someone with whom I ought to talk. Being seated near the back of the room allowed me to reach the door before almost anyone else, and there I waited for my unsuspecting pray.

I cleared my throat as she walked past, and flashed a broad smile with just enough of a dangerous edge. "Excuse me, Young Lady!"

She took note; glancing up at me and flushing mildly. I suspected she would. Middle-aged women love being referred to as "Young Lady".

"Yes?" Her smile was sincere, if nervous.

"I just wanted to let you know how impressed I was with the questions you asked Mr. Mason. I've read his work pertaining to communication with the deceased, and his accomplishments are impressive. If I were as brave as you, I'd have asked him to channel my recently departed Grandma." I looked down with a rueful smile. My 94-year-old Granny was alive, but riddled with dementia. I wish someone *could* channel her long-absent lucidity.

The woman looked at me, eyes aglow with feverish enthusiasm. "Yes! He is great, isn't he? And a good family man as well." She held up a copy of some book of his called "Coming into the Light," and flipped it open to reveal a signature on the inner cover. "I met him a few years ago at a Barnes and Noble book signing, but I don't think he remembered me just now."

Poor lady. If it weren't for her two thousand-dollar suit or her delusional behaviour, I'd never have remembered her either. I shook my head in a display of deep regret, and shifted my considerable body weight against the hallway wall. "I, too, was once a good family man. Alas, my wife took me for everything I had, and then took off."

The lady looked at me genuine sympathy. Despite her age, there was an element of true naivety to her. Perfect. "I'm truly sorry."

"You're so kind." I shifted myself until I was fully upright and took a few paces down the corridor, motioning for her to follow if she wanted. "Your husband is a very lucky man." I'd noticed her unadorned ring finger, of course.

"You're a flatterer." She covered her mouth with a demure hand and tittered. "I'm afraid I haven't got a husband." She must have enjoyed my flattery, for she began to walk with me. "I'm a widow."

"That's very sad, Miss…"

"Cutlass. Alice Cutlass."

"Well, Miss Cutlass, would you like to join me for drinks and maybe a bite to eat?"

I was pretty sure she batted her eyelashes. A sorry sight, but a good sign. "If you're paying."

Well, fuck. This one still had a sense of entitlement. No matter; I could swing a few meals. Besides, Alice was skinny. She'd probably feel full after a salad. "Depends where we're going. Do you like Italian?"

Later that night, as we lingered by candle light over bottles of wine and towering plates of pasta, I realised just how deceptive appearances could be. Waiflike as she was, Alice could down a triple portion of Fettuccini Alfredo without issue. I had always been a good cook, at least when it came to basic bachelor chow like pasta, so it stood to reason that this might be the key to her heart (and pocketbook).

Miss Cutlass described herself as a "professional traveler and liver of life". She seemed too religious, and not quite attractive enough, to work as a high-end call-girl, so she was probably independently wealthy. Maybe she had inherited her fortune from her late husband, a doctor who'd passed away three years prior. She was certainly available to travel. While she spoke of having a home on the north coast of Ohio, most of the tales she told were of adventures out of state and country.

For the remainder of the convention, we were inseparable. We attended talks and workshops together, and even went to the formal dance held in the Hilton's grand ballroom. Through the nights, my newfound lady friend kept me occupied in other ways, putting true effort into my pleasure in the manner of a truly desperate – and grateful – female. By week's end, I felt what seemed like a genuine attachment to the poor creature.

So connected did I feel that when we were intimate, her descended breasts seemed to perk up before my eyes, and her facial age spots appeared to recede into her primary peachy complexion. In personality she was perhaps a touch offbeat, but there were moments of astounding insight and intelligence relating to the sciences. She was the first person I'd met since completing my degree who could hold her own in conversation about subatomic particles and the principles of thermodynamics.

I rationalised this predicament might have risen due to long-term loneliness. This was the deepest relationship I'd formed since my failed marriage, and admittedly the procession of interchangeable one-night stands had provided little genuine companionship. As Alice and I shared brunch at the nearest Original Pancake House (my treat once more, but I understood the importance of short-term investments where long-term payoff would result), a strange idea occurred to me. Miss Cutlass had a permanent home base, but did not seem to be in any great hurry to return.

"Alice," I began, "I know you must have a lot to get back to in Ohio, but first…would you like to stop by Vancouver and stay for a bit?" I took a few nervous bites of Dutch Apple Pancake, sipped my coffee, and nervously awaited her response.

"I'm flattered," she smiled, fiddling with her napkin. "But you wouldn't want an old lady like me puttering about. What would people say about an eligible young man shacking up with a 52-year-old woman"

I clasped her hand. "They'll say they're happy we both managed to find love."

* * *

We drove back to Vancouver together, sharing music and making memories all along the way. Surprisingly, Alice was familiar with some of my favourite J-pop and symphonic metal bands. "Of course I like Nightwish. Everyone on Earth does. I've been a big fan since '04," she once commented nonchalantly. Here was an old lady who, despite appearances, refused to live in the past.

Our time together was not *all* sunshine and roses. There were exchanges which necessitated my putting the lady in her place. When she commented on my eating habits, for instance, I let her know that her face might look more youthful if she were to put on a few pounds. I also made sure to hit her with a neg when she became overconfident about her appearance. She may have had an enviable figure, but her skin was looser and drier than that of a younger woman. I had to drive home the point that she was lucky to have me if I were going to gain an upper hand in this situation.

We spent the next month at my condo and environs. Alice seemed extremely low-maintenance; content to hang about my house offering sensuous pleasures and playing games online. She was mostly a PC gamer, which left the Xbox 360 and PS3 constantly available for my enjoyment. Not once did she complain about being taken too few places, having too few material comforts, or any other trivial matters.

I began to introduce her to my less costly pastimes, such as bird-watching, and convinced her to sign on under me in the LIVE business, which was reassuring. She could be convinced to loosen her purse-strings. I'd have to ease her in to acting as my provider slowly; bit by bit. With any hope I could convince her by the beginning of the following month. Otherwise, we would be without electricity, and our heat would be shut off just as the temperature began to dip.

Alice became a big hit at my local CakeMakers meetings. At first the age difference was difficult for some people to digest. Being overweight has always kept me looking young, and much to her chagrin Miss Cutlass was frequently mistaken for my mother. Once she got to know those in my chapter, however, and impressed them with her knowledge of matters physical and meta-, their hearts opened to our coupledom.

At the start of October, as feared, I received a letter warning of an impending disconnect from our electric service. I lacked the funds to pay for even one month of continued energy, so I supposed this was as good a time as any to ask Alice if she would spring for next month's utility bills.

I asked her that evening, over a meal by candlelight which I hoped I'd be able to continue using out of romantic whimsy rather than blind necessity. She glanced down at the floor, and paused. I wondered if the turndown at the corners of her mouth was due to some sort of internal conflict or the simple breakdown of collagen and elastin in the skin following the menopause.

"Well, er, I..." she seemed awfully hesitant. Then she reached into her pocket (for she was wearing a clever sort of knit dress which included them), and then extended a closed palm. When it opened, I was somewhat surprised to see a magnificent ring, bearing a largish heart-shaped constellation of diamonds and rimmed in other assorted jewels. "If I agreed, would you marry me?"

Jackpot! I could scarcely believe the elaborately-bejeweled ring she was offering. This would indeed be the end of my economic woes – and, it seems, it would come with a coincidental side of companionship. I immediately dropped my silverware, my half-eaten Commodore Tso's Chicken forgotten. "YES!!" I leapt from my seat and bounded around the table to hug my savior. I swung her around – she was light as a helium balloon in my arms. Too late, I realised this was the sort of enthusiasm I'd long known better than to show toward the opposite sex. I crossed my arms and leaned against the wall, assuming my trademarked cocky smile. "I mean, okay, if you think you can handle me."

Alice got our electricity situation straightened out the next day. The day after that, we found a cleric and obtained our marriage certificate. Sadly, a quick bit of research online told me keeping her in

Canada would require me to fall under a certain income bracket, which would necessitate employment or a second stab at blackmail. But I wasn't worried. My wife was loaded.

That afternoon we discussed the situation, and Alice invited me to join her in Ohio. Spousal visas, it seemed, were easier to obtain in the US than anywhere else. She suggested we sell my condo, since I would no longer need a local place to say. I admitted it was a great idea, and made an appointment at my bank to discuss putting the condo on the market. Within two weeks we had a buyer, and before the month was through we'd received a cool $300,000 CAN deposit.

*   *   *

After an action-packed, but cramped, 3 days on the road, we found ourselves on the stretch of 2 East which Alice said led to her hometown of Painesville. Cleveland's east side greeted us with a dense snow storm and slippery roads courtesy of my dear country directly to the north sending its so-called "Lake Effect Snow". I'd been warned, but hadn't expected it to arrive right on cue. Though both of us were annoyed with spending our waking hours in a cramped car, we took things slow. Better safe than dead.

Finally we disembarked from the freeway, and Alice directed me through a few hairpin turns. Finally we arrived at a nondescript brick building which was protected by a threatening-looking fence. Several shady looking characters, mostly young and male, hung about the grounds.

"Well, this is it," said Alice, motioning me into the care park. "Home sweet home".

She had to be joking. The place looked like a project. My wife didn't seem bothered. I followed her into a drab-looking lobby area in industrial lime green and gray. At the room's center, a chubby and rough looking lady sat behind a desk. She requested ID.

"Alice, formerly Cutlass," my wife announced, placing her driver's license and credit card (why was the latter necessary?) on the desk for our greeter's perusal. "And this is my husband."

"Ah, Miss Cutlass. You haven't been around lately. We were worried. Don't fear. There are rooms available. Thank you for returning our card. By the way, would you happen to have that suit Mr. Brooks loaned you? He and the other folks at Dressed for Success were afraid it was gone forever!"

"Tell Mike he can pick it up at his convenience, Donna." she aimed a winning smile at the lady behind the desk, then winked at me. "I'll need to keep the ring, though."

"Don't worry your pretty little head. It's only a cubic zirconium." She looked in my direction and gasped, "Uh-oh. Erm..."

I felt ill. Everything was coming into place! The guard lady narrowed her eyes, looking me over with an expression I couldn't read. "Welcome to Wyatt Home for the Transient, Sir. Before you can stay here, we'll need the following documents...."

fin

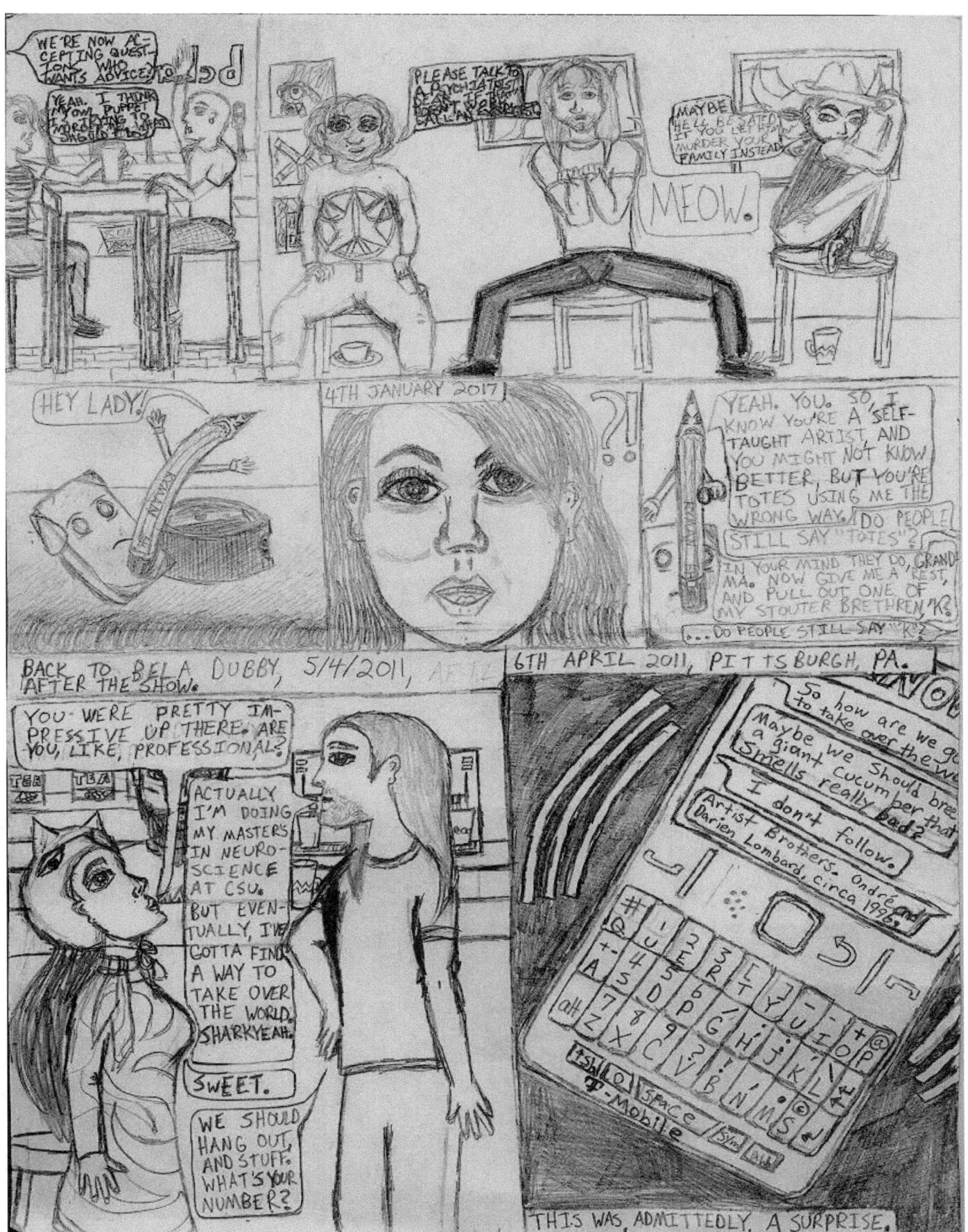

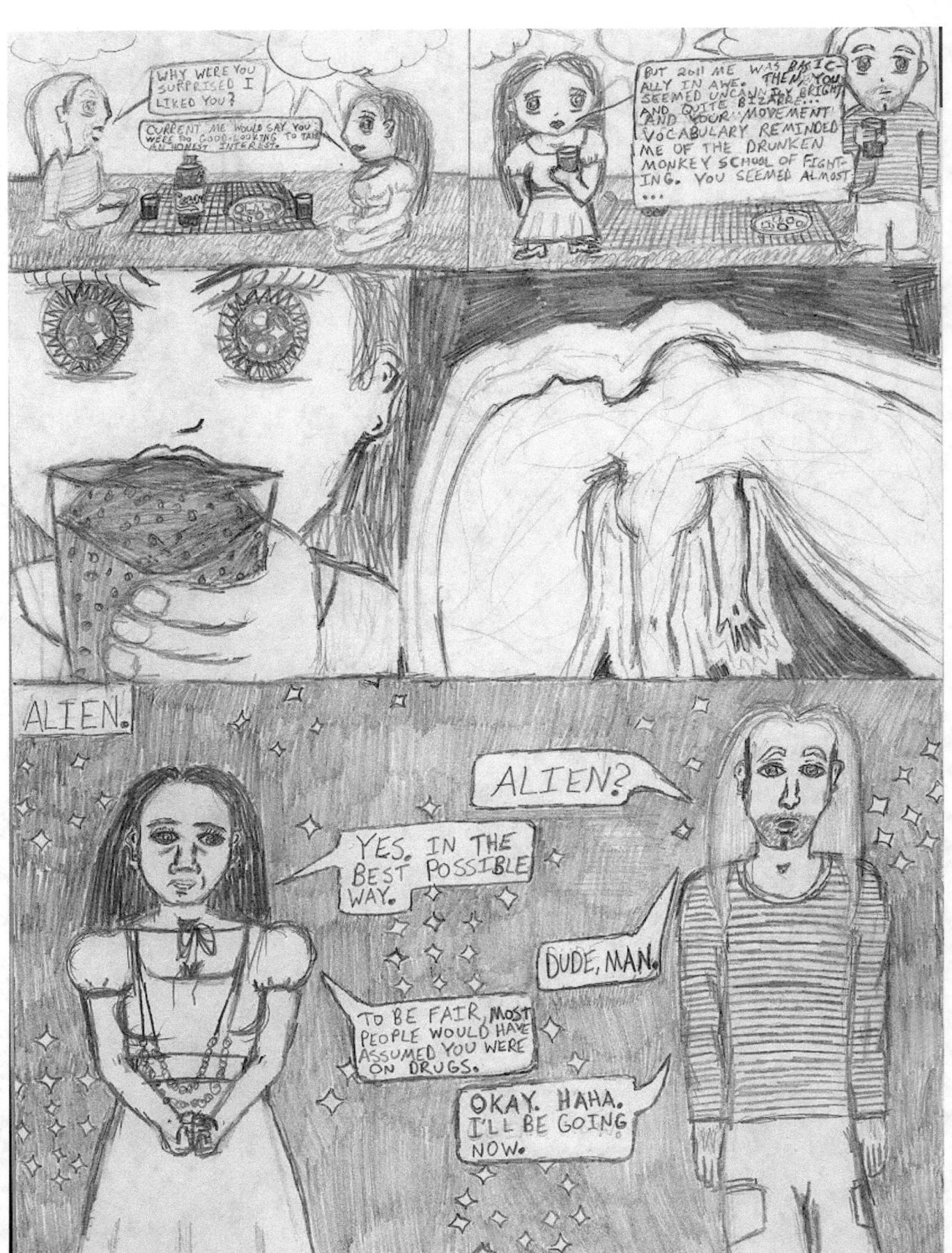

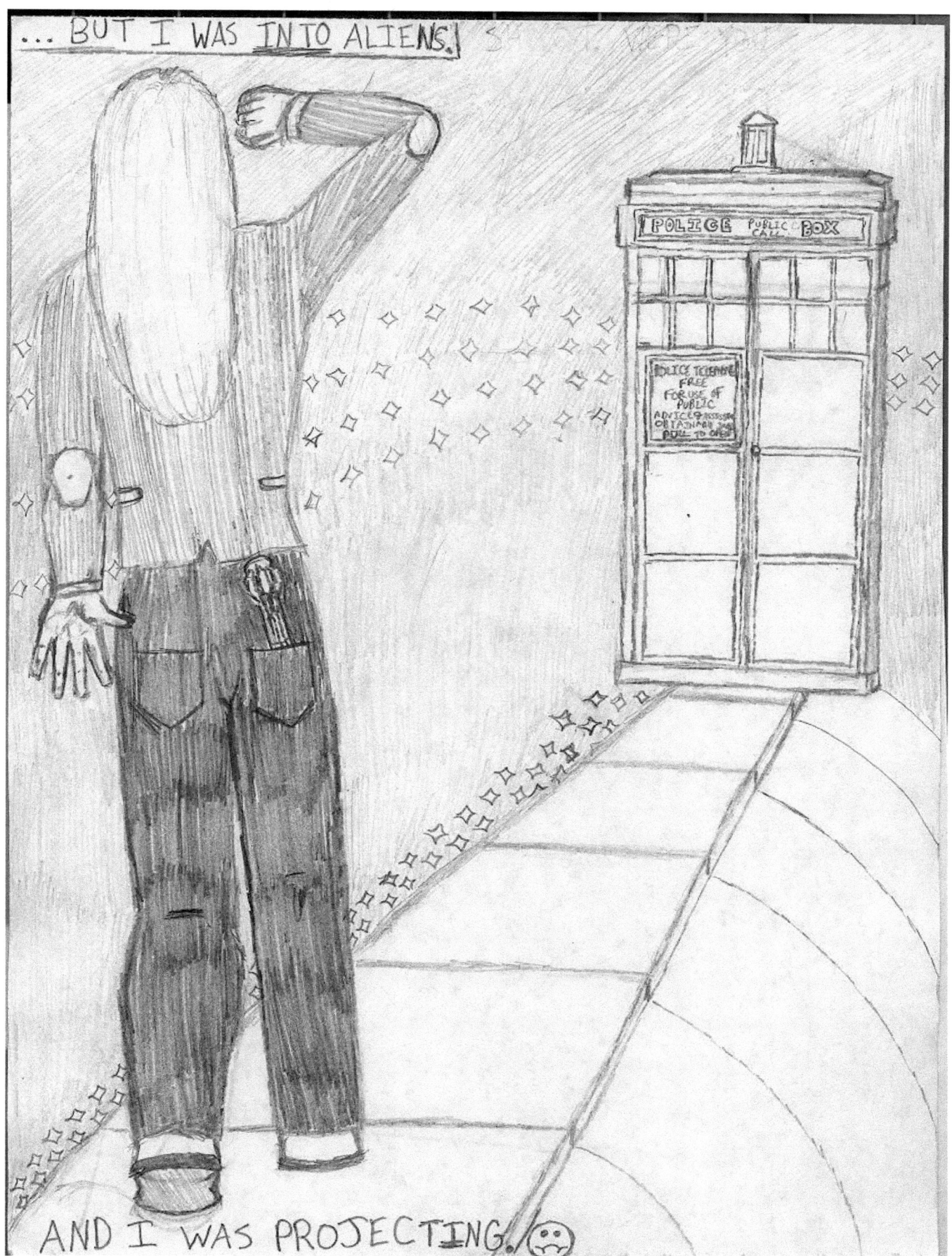

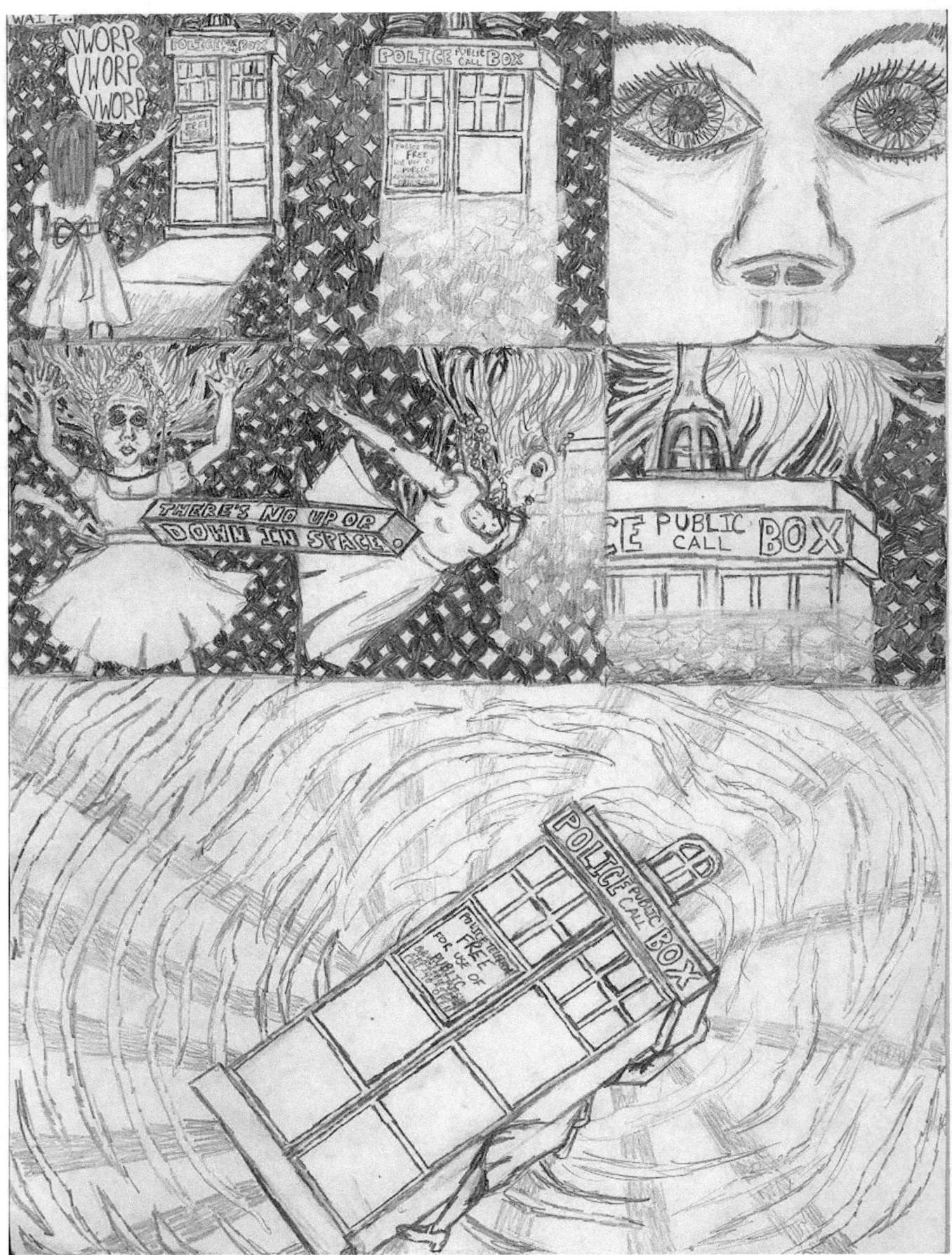

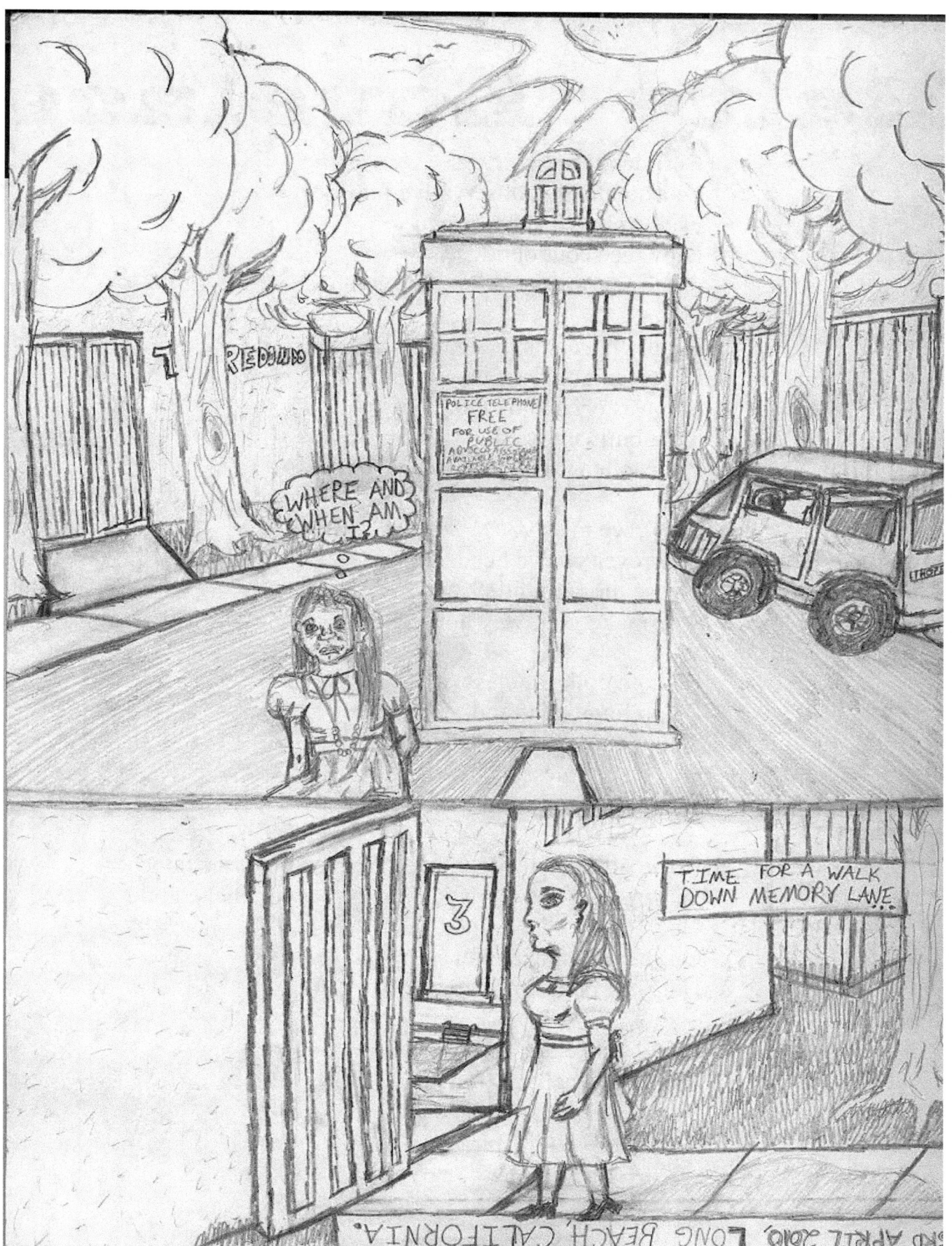

Betty Lovelace

Born in Nebraska, 1923
Of a staunchly conservative family
Friday church suppers and
Brownie scout outings
the firm cornerstones of her youth

Beauty pageants in Kearney and Lincoln
Managed not to let insults and mockery sink in
She was chosen by God
To submit and wed
Prior to length of the tooth.

Betty, we miss you.
Wherever you've headed,
Please turn around,
And make your way home.

Lincoln college, class of 1945
BA in linguistics and feeling alive.
"Did you find a husband,
Our littlest blessing?"
Curious minds want to know.

Roy's off in Europe, and Joe's joined the priesthood
Serving as good Christian men; now you make good
On your divine purpose,
Our beautiful daughter
Help our poor family to grow.

Betty, where are you?
Momma is calling.
Daddy is mad,
And Paul's on the phone.

Betty Lovelace (cont.)

Three children, delightful, with nappies to change,
Distressed cries to sooth, play-dates to arrange
Meals prepared, floors to scrub
A woman's work never ends
And isn't that the greatest joy?

Left the cornfields, 1954
For a plane higher and offering more
Societies rebuilt
And enemies vanquished,
Compassionate, brilliant change,

Betty, come home please,
Raise up your children
Honour your vows, dear,
to family and God.

Dropped off in the city, 1996,
Temporally displaced and from the sticks
Silver shoes, graffiti,
New York City, AIDS
Intellectuals, Queens

Wonder what she's doing in times more recent
How does she react to an era indecent?
Identity politics,
triggering world,
Dystopic 2017?

Betty, you're out there
Hear us, we're calling
Heaven or Hell
Hear us from far away.

Betty, we trust that
You're not gone forever,
But Betty, we miss you –
So come home to stay.

Underground

Anxiety drowns in fear,
A stifling suffocation
That burns in the mind

Trapped in a cage certainly
One composed entirely
Of constraints on time

Buried alive underground
Last heard screaming desperately
Forgotten and gone

Crying for angelic wings
Tearfully follow along
To the haunting song

*"Love lies long cross the ocean
Reaching out with no success
Grasping empty air*

*"Hear the sound vibrate through ground
Let it offer hope and strength
When life's tough to bear."*

Deep in cold isolation
Shuddering very slightly
Afraid to emerge

Aerated nozzle focus
Swift deterioration
Funereal dirge

Is there life beyond the soil?
Only safe, sweet darkness here
Round this slab of stone

Though leagues afar and absurd
Dulcet tones heard from
Mate's faraway throne.

*"Love lies long cross the ocean
Reaching out with no success
Grasping empty air*

*"Hear the sound vibrate through ground
Let it offer hope and strength
When life's tough to bear."*

It did, and it does.

Home

Safety. Security. Seclusion.
Twelve-by-fifteen-by-ten-foot cube
Of solitude, a modest castle
Built on the foundations of
Those beneath.
Dense paper jungles of literature,
Vibrant image, and implements
To introduce either
To a world which they'll never view.
Cushions of fabrics; silks and satins;
Lace, organza, and taffeta
Leather, pleather and vinyl
Like a Victorian aristo and
An alterna-kid from the nineties
Collided at the airport;
Their belongings flying and
Settling into luxurious mountains.
Hundreds of shoes, soles aglow
Recalling avenues
Trod or run or struggled
Down leaving them
Worn, but wiser each step
Huddle for warmth in
Their mass grave,

Home (cont.)

Peering outward
T'where charcoal and
Lighter fluid wait,
Alongside a cooler,
Dreaming of summers yet-to-come
Beneath battered suitcases,
Memories lay buried,
Each photograph a portal to the past
A distant place, a foreign face,
Friendship long-gone
But never forgotten
Even as the documents
Of life's bureaucracies
Grow impregnably skyward
Even as cosmetics and
Skin-care supplements
Pile up in the corners
As plushies stand guard
And candles cast flickering
Shades of warmth
Under floral siblings
Living and dead
Upon the shelf,
Under a ceiling of glowing stars...
A happy, hyggelyge home.

Worldly

I first traveled northward, and learned
the virtues of patience, kindness,
and compassion.

In the south my lessons
were attentiveness, grace and precision.

Traveling west provided a lesson
in dedication, faithfulness and love.

The Force 10 eastern wind blew past,
leaving in its wake rubble rearranged by
perception, prudence, and caution.

Unusual features adorn this map;
mountains and valleys cut by networks
of crystalline streams wending
their ways toward destinations
puzzle-imperfect but peaceful.

For a Dear (Former) Friend

We met while I dated your friend,
With whom you shared a home.
You were cooler not only than me,
But than I might ever hope to be.
Tattooed, pierced, and well-versed in punk,
With rainbow-bright hair and
While a scowl too-cool-for-school-or-anything-else
Adorned your pallid face,
Mystique graced your back, signifying
The possibility of change and transformation.
The lithe lengths of your Southern necessities
Were woven into some yogic pose or other
As you worked on your latest masterpiece,
A paintbrush in one hand and remote in the other
As Netflix flickered from
Supernatural to footage of the Distillers.
You were tough, and bold, and fiercely clever,
Outspoken, a staunch defender and
Mighty fighter for right
You were absolutely everything I wished to be.
Never in millenia'd I feel you'd see me
As a friend, but that's the relationship
We came to have...
Though your peculiar mate and I
Severed ties, our love remained
And grew, renewing my faith
In love and life and humanity
Together we embarked upon
Adventures near and far and
Our feelings grew...eventually,
I began to open up to you.
But the floodgates flew wide open,
And too weak to seal them,
I allowed you to drown in
That deluge of tears and self-pity and neuroses
You needed to breathe, but could find no relief
Save apart from me.
So you wthdrew,
And until I renew,
You are a soul I was lucky to know.
So peacefully you go...
Though a piece of you remains
And helps me to refrain
From repeating old mistakes.

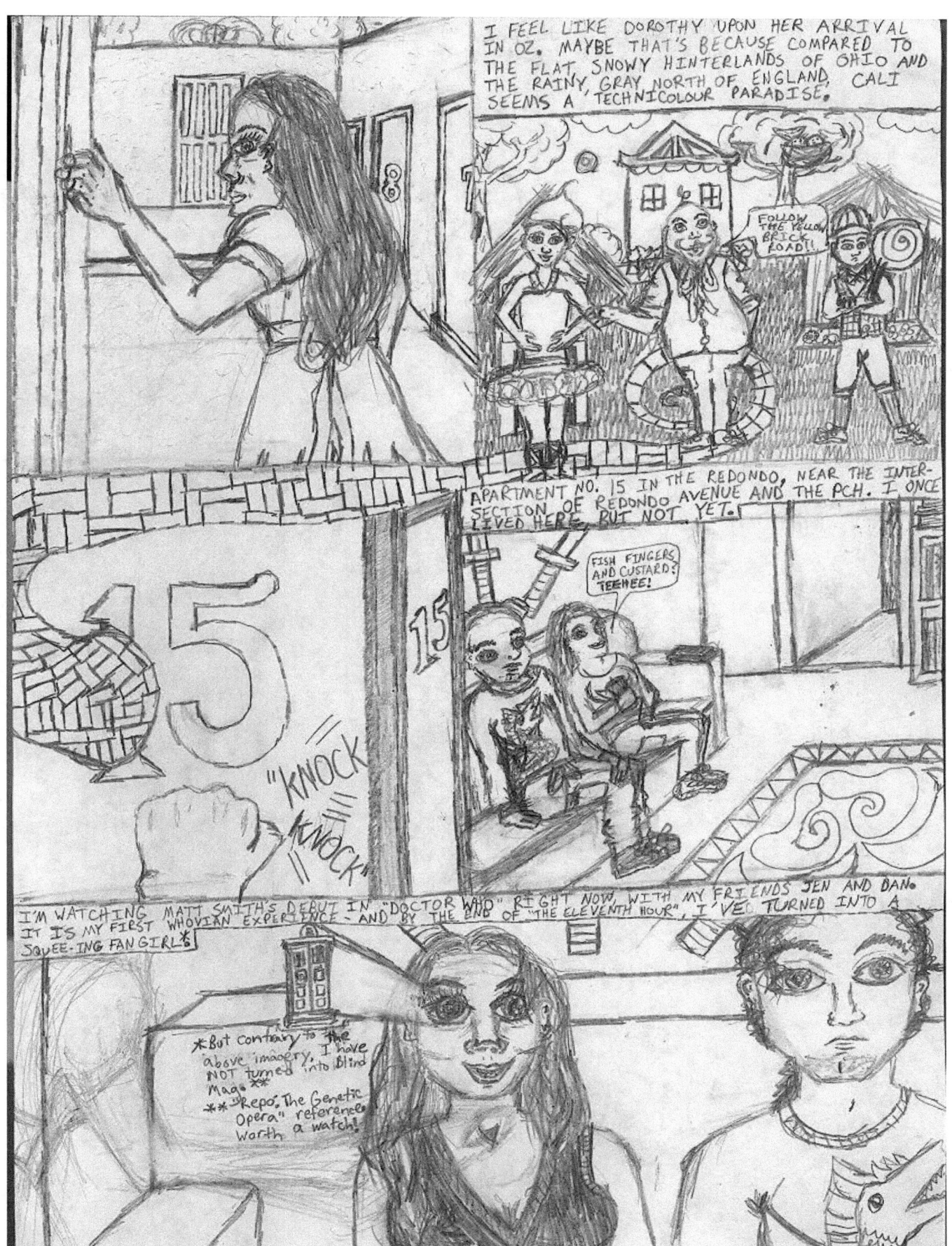

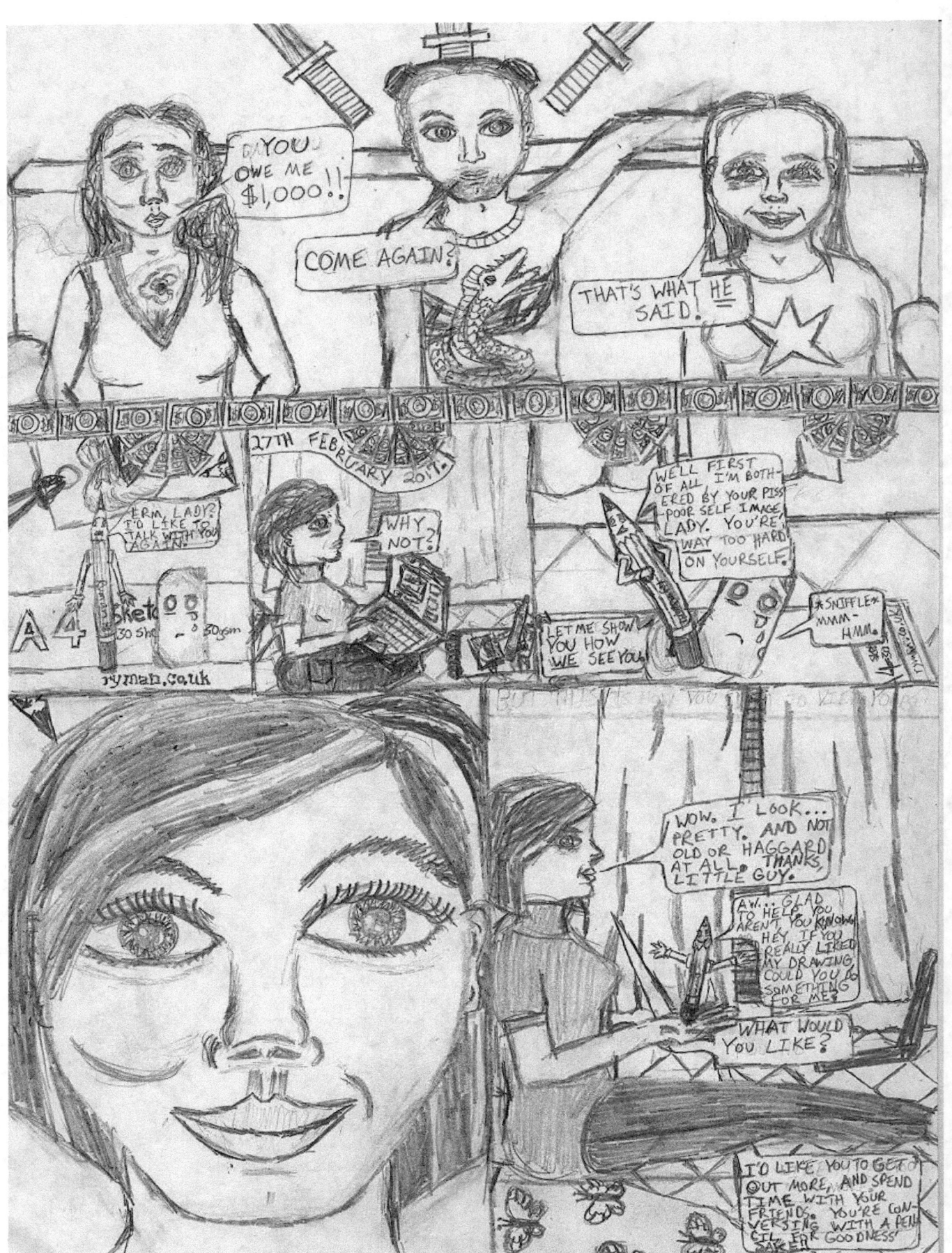

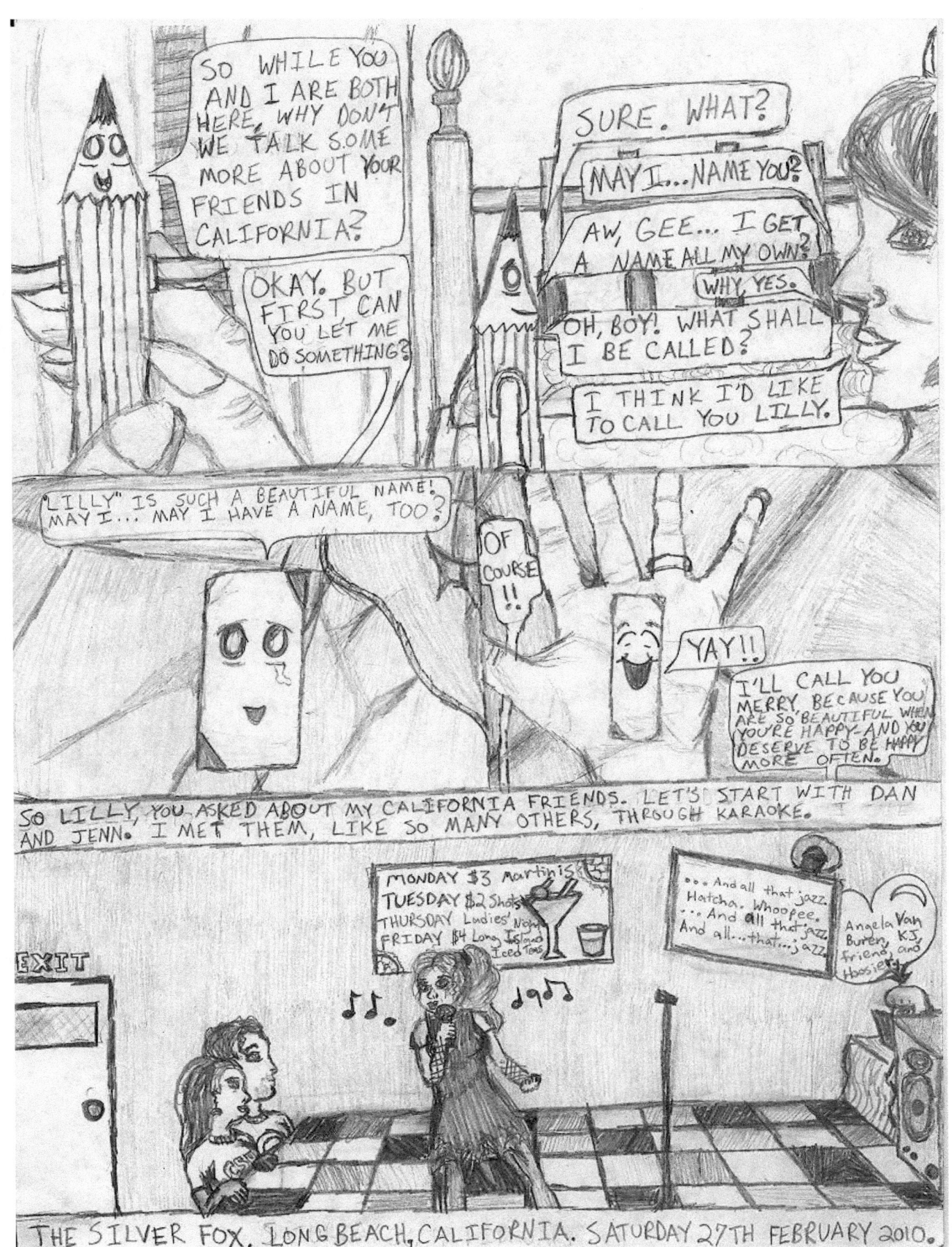

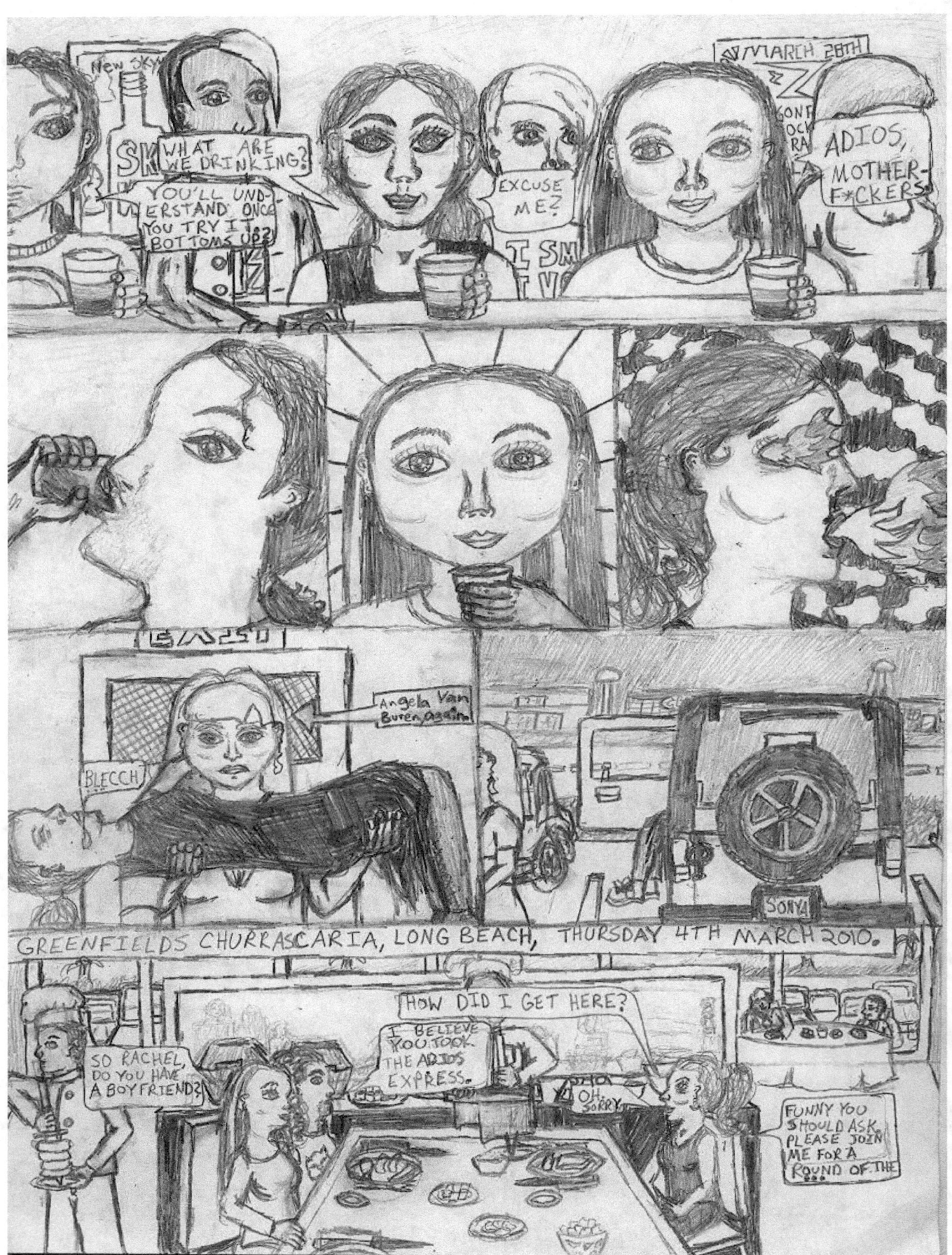

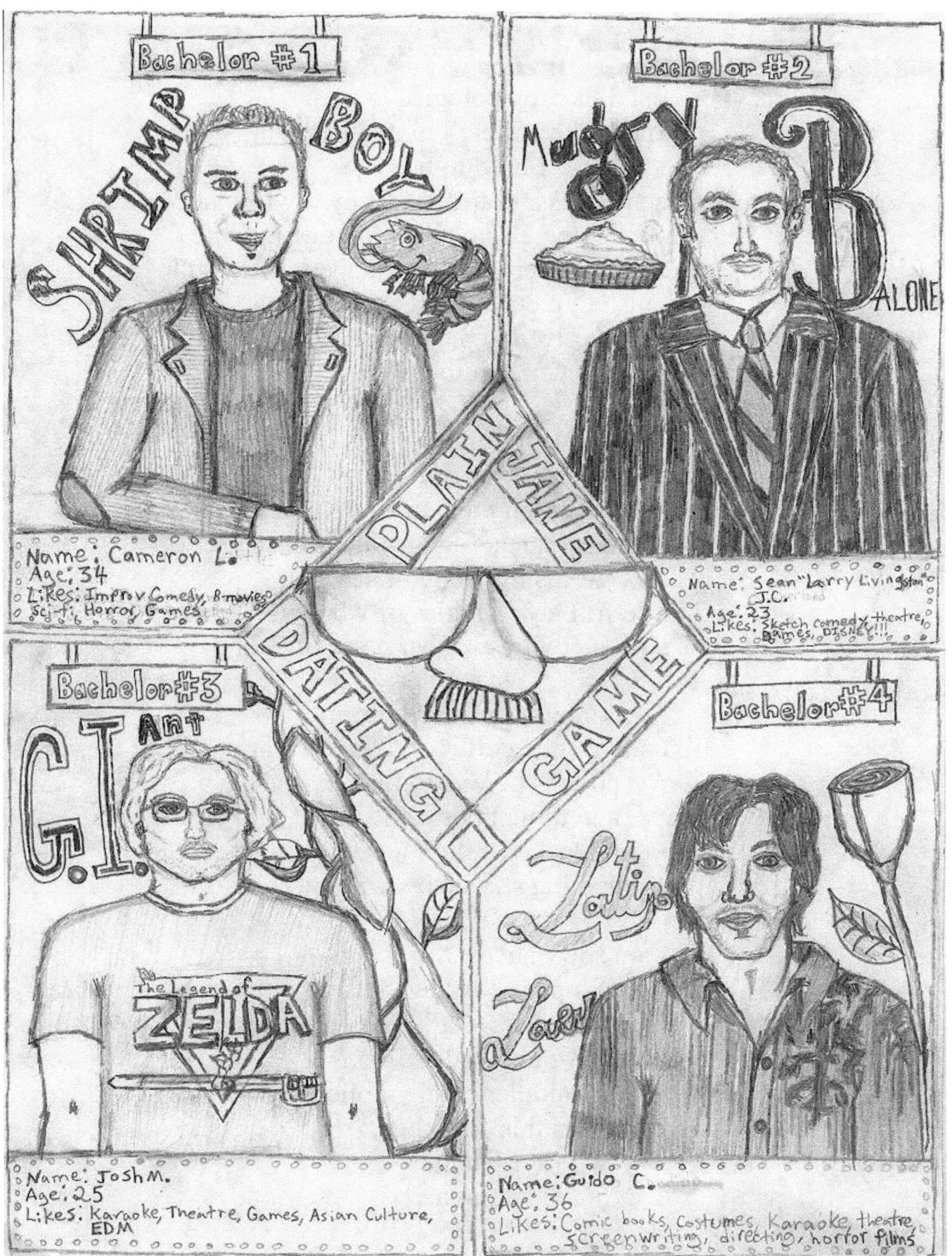

Arrest

I'd like to apologise to you,
And make it clear I'm not the girl
I used to be.
But you see me as a brainless, filthy lowlife, no?
You think that there's no changing one like me.
I chastise myself every day my misbegotten youth
Or misbegotten young(er) adulthood.
Curse 15th September 2010.
Curse it to hell.
While only six point five years in the past
A lifetime away
In someone else's story
Someone who has felt the fear of imminent death
As cold steel rests against their head
And sings show tunes
And rattles off etymologies of words to cope
As she is led like a cheap piece of beef
To slaughter
Caught in a terror trap
To enhance the coffer of a few fat cats
And yet she was to blame...
She was petty, and thoughtless, and naive, and young,
And lacked common sense.
Something she shares with me,
To a degree.
I am sorry she so affronted you.
So please forgive me,
Mr. Anderson. And Mrs. Ball. And Mr. Rodriguez.
Forgive me, and set me free
From another bleak oubliette
In this wretched.
Mental.
Prison

Aspiring Song

Far, far too literal/
With no sense of poetry or metaphor/
I'm waging war/
With the voices in my head,/
Issue from the heart instead/
And bring back the flow/
From which I've fled.

Why won't you humour me/
With symbolic imag'ry and colour?/
You're such a bor-/ing
Brain when you trail off
And bog down the mind with moth/-balls
Which won't evaporate/
It's a turnoff

And I've no chorus/
For the dinosauress/
Who's writing chose to
Pen a crippled song/
First steps aren't easy, though
I'm more than nothing...
So how can you tell me
My existence is wrong?

My literary devices
Are illiterate and oh so shallow
Not much below
Surface of the raging sea
Obscuring creativity
And stealing time
I'm so inclined

To write a chorus
Though this tune seems porous
I still feel that
It's hobbling on one leg
Though first steps aren't easy,
I am gaining traction
For one more extension
I'll be gauche enough to beg

I'll infuse your world with sunshine
And I'll free you from the dark
And I'll clear away the cobwebs
Once I find that inner spark
I will free your loving passions
And your inner child too
Just give me a chance at living
'Cause it's all I'd like to do...

Opening the mental channels
Maybe ending better than the start
Playing its part
Putting on a mask of comp/etence
And hoping you won't stomp
Its lifeblood out
And what about

Another chorus
Erupting with for-(uce)
To compensate
For disappointing you
Though first steps aren't easy,
I'll stride out with style
Making an impression
Before bidding adieu

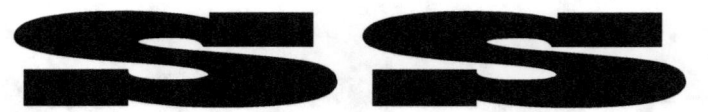

Some would describe you as needing a beard/
And others as just plain weird/
But nothing could stop you
From eclipsing the moon that night.

You pawed and you purred; inquisitively mewed/
You were one Jesus-looking dude/
Oh you were a weirdo,
But performing you shone so bright.

Tonight let us drink to a friend, though unparted/
Our life together ended before it started/
A neuroscientist made off with a brain
And it was left humming a dull, gray refrain.

To Halloween parties and days at the Zoo/
To building a dream anew/
To discov'ring new friends,
And uncharted paths in life/

To Southern Plantations; events grand and small/
Cinderella at her Royal Ball/
To laughter and music/
With one's goal as a future wife/

After five years her memories left unfaded/
Rose-filtered though their host's long since become jaded/
Their magical unicorn's flying on high,
While they remain earthbound with eyes toward the sky.

Dorian Gray Hair

Crows' feet cross your sagging temples
Train tracks etched 'cross your forehead
Your glabella's got angry elevens
And your lips are thinning, love.
Your malar pads show much descent
Nasal tip is drooping, swell!
Receding salty hairline above
Patchy and archless eyebrows.
Happy, innocent expression
Belies your internal rot
But not
The onset of middle age.
Better dig out that old portrait, dear,
'Cause it's doing you no favours.
Dorian Gray, you are no more.
Dorian Gray, you are no more.

Aiding Salvation

The world is a leviathan
Waiting to pull you below tide
Grind up your insides
One less leech for which
to provide,
So ride it out and
Stand to the side
And don't be denied
The right to remain alive.

Try and fight the power,
But how are you to shout aloud
When a bout with the law
Could leave you without
A mouth to pronounce
Profound outrage
Don't bring it down,
But drown it out
So you can thrive.

                            Stay on the sidelines
Where it's safe, and try not to stray
Too far away; be a free agent
But wisely afraid;
Best put the brakes on
What you say
Lest it flail, or fail
And fade in vain
Before it can arrive.

Create at the edge of sight,
Because it is better to do;
Prove your worth and never
Let the world roofie you –
Let your message move
The masses who might go mute;
Become a muse
Through tune or verse;
Build worlds toward which to strive.

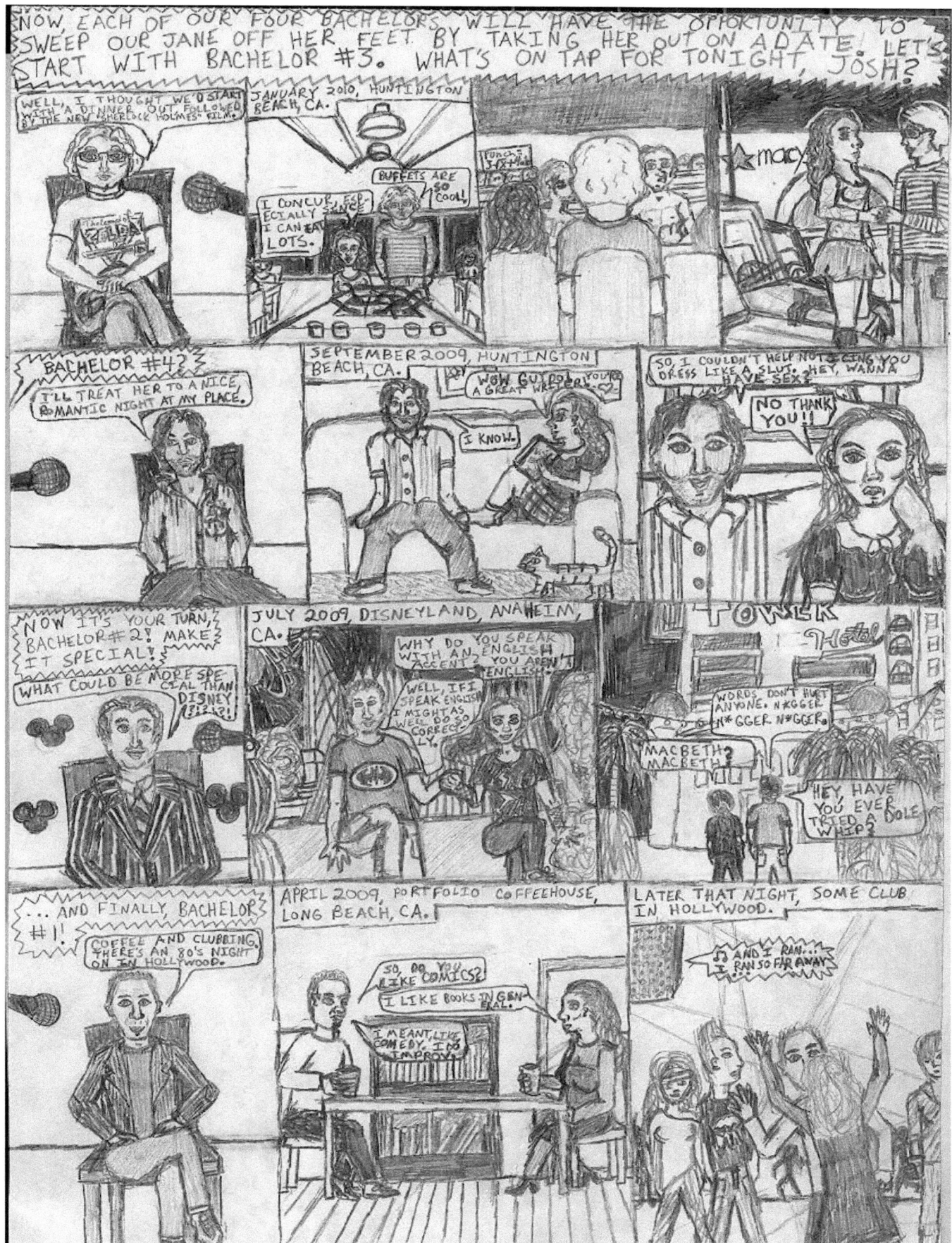

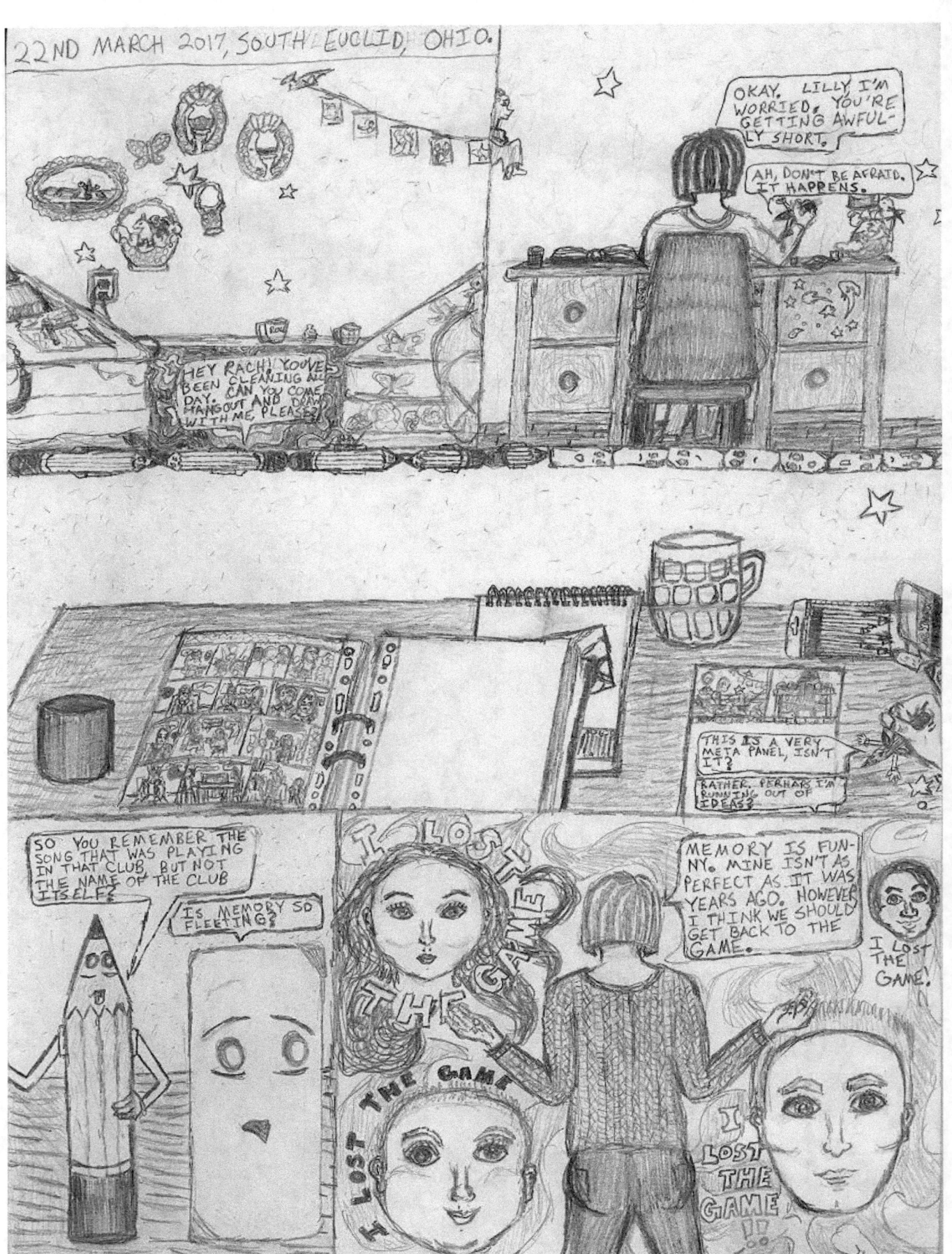

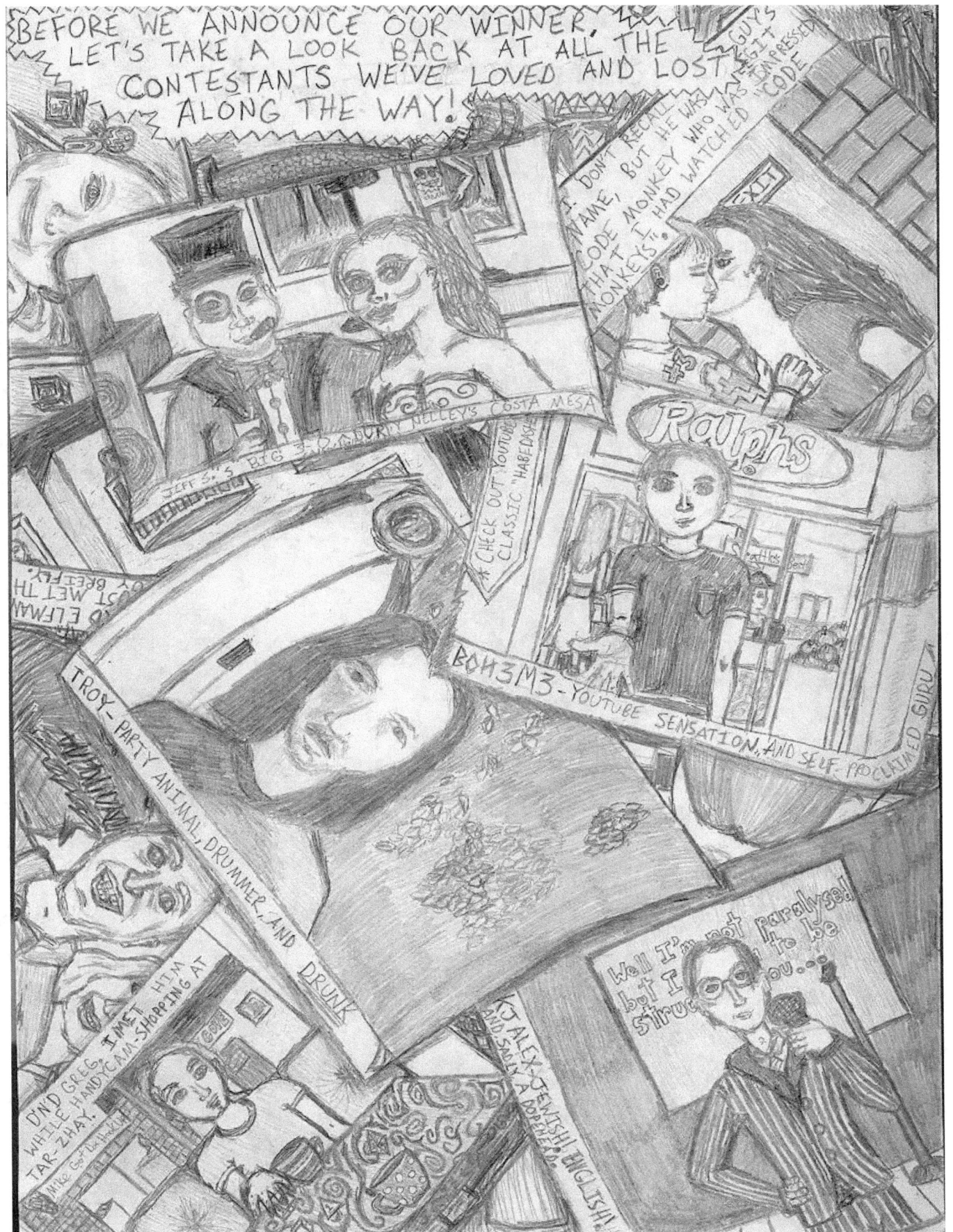

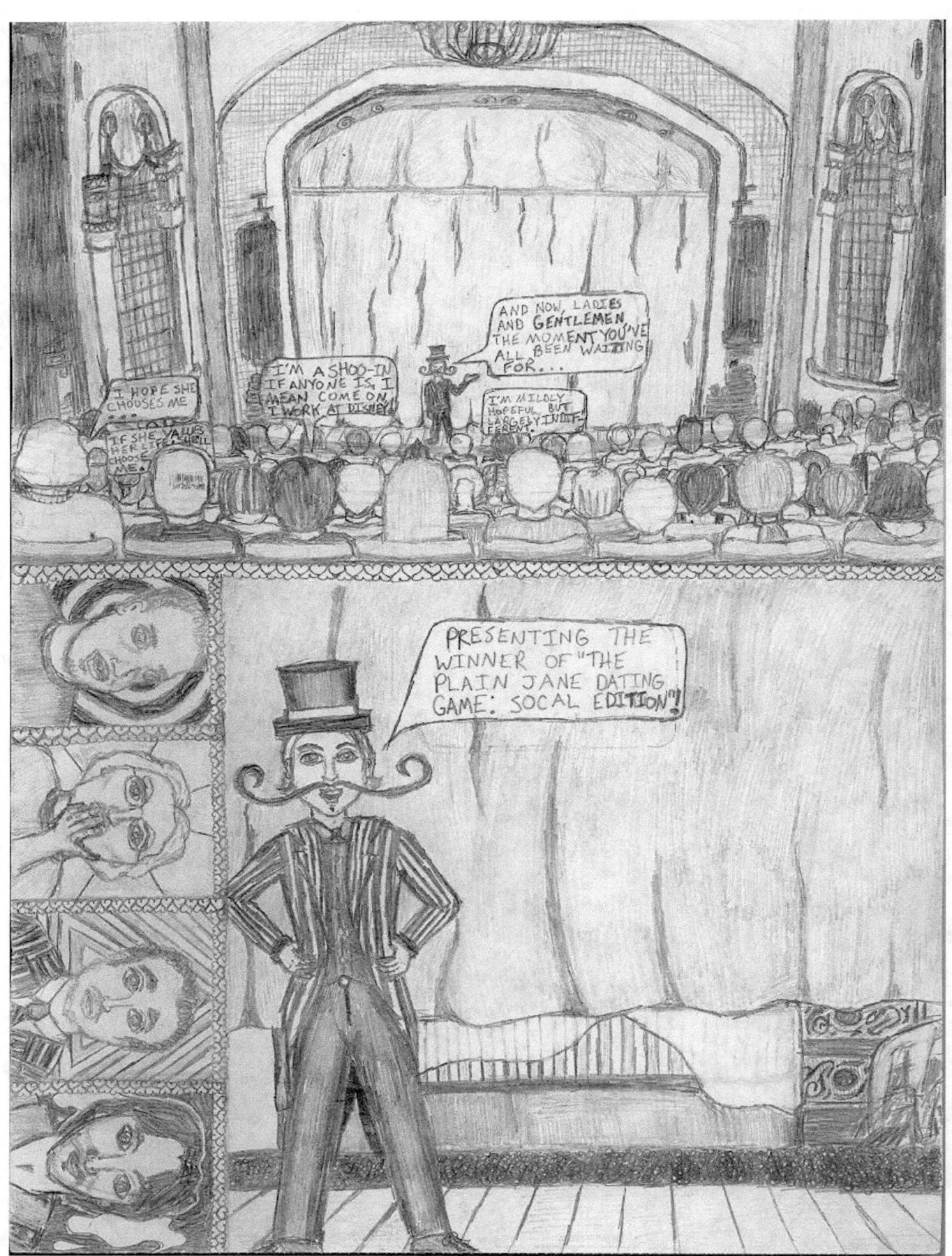

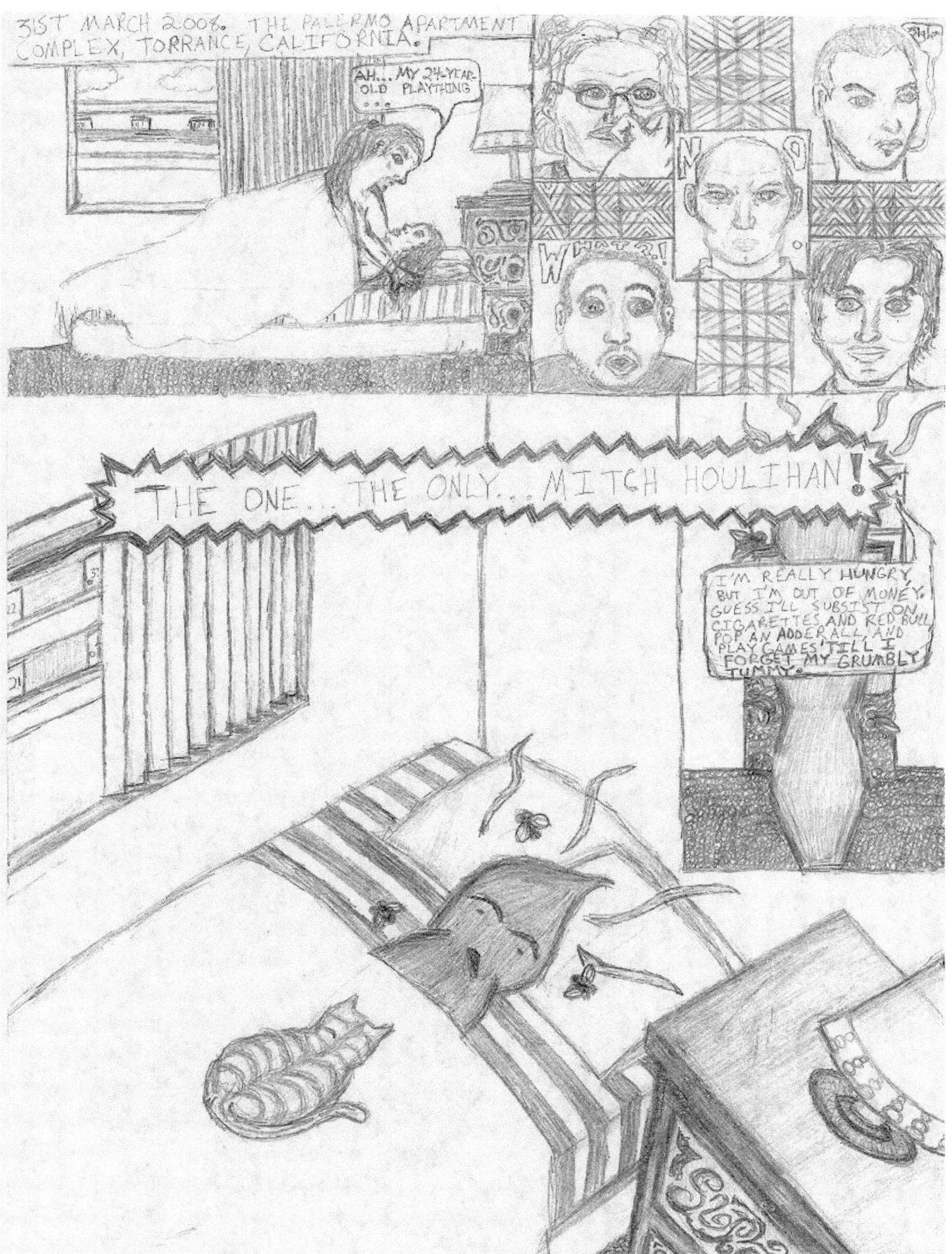

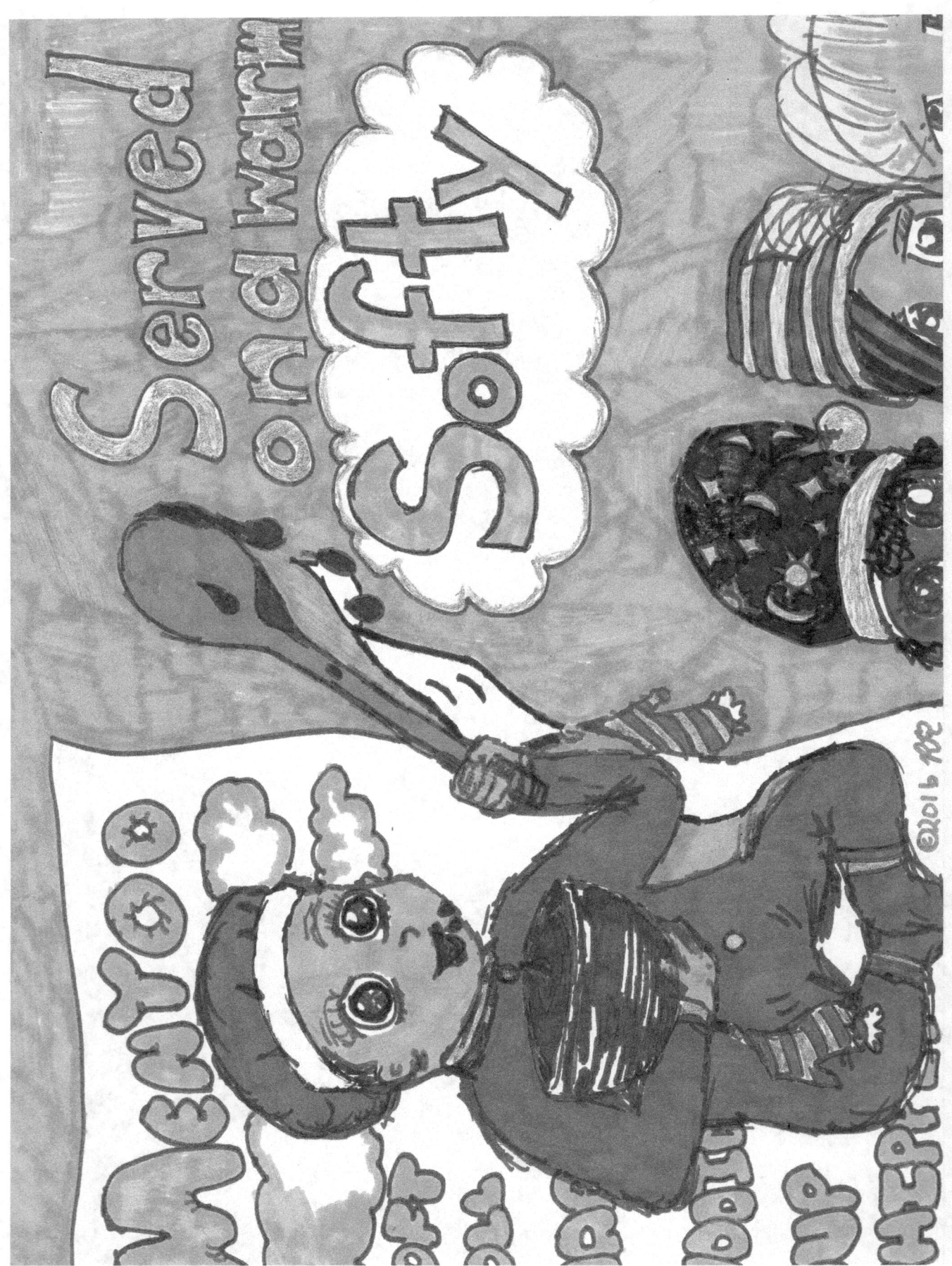

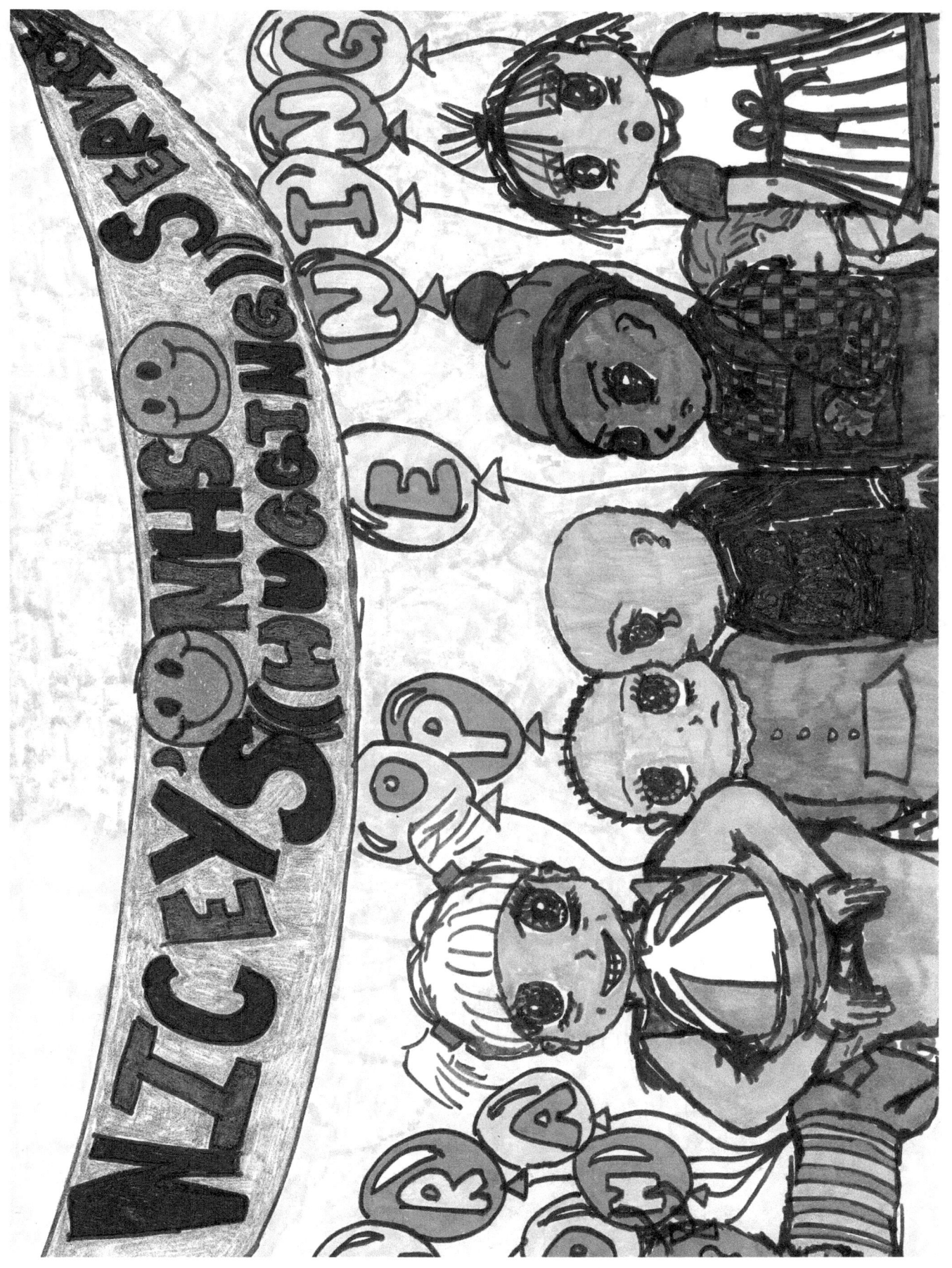

Belonging

Do you feel alienated,
Separate from the human throng?
Well, you can come on over here, 'cause you belong.

When you think you just aren't good enough,
And get everything wrong,
Please take comfort in the fact that you belong.

Know you're loved
And know you're skilled
And there's no limit
If you're strong-willed
You're worthwhile
You've earned your place
And you're a gift
To the human race.

Have you been abused or bullied,
Feel like singing your swan song?
Please do bless us with your life, cause you belong.

If you feel like giving up,
Please take my hand and come along,
Anyone worth knowing knows that you belong.

Anyone worth knowing knows,
Life may not smell like a rose,
Though tempestuous writhe its throes
Below a sky of raven crows
And its normies speak in prose
Reality's a sob'ring dose
So come here; I'll hold you close
'Cause you belong!

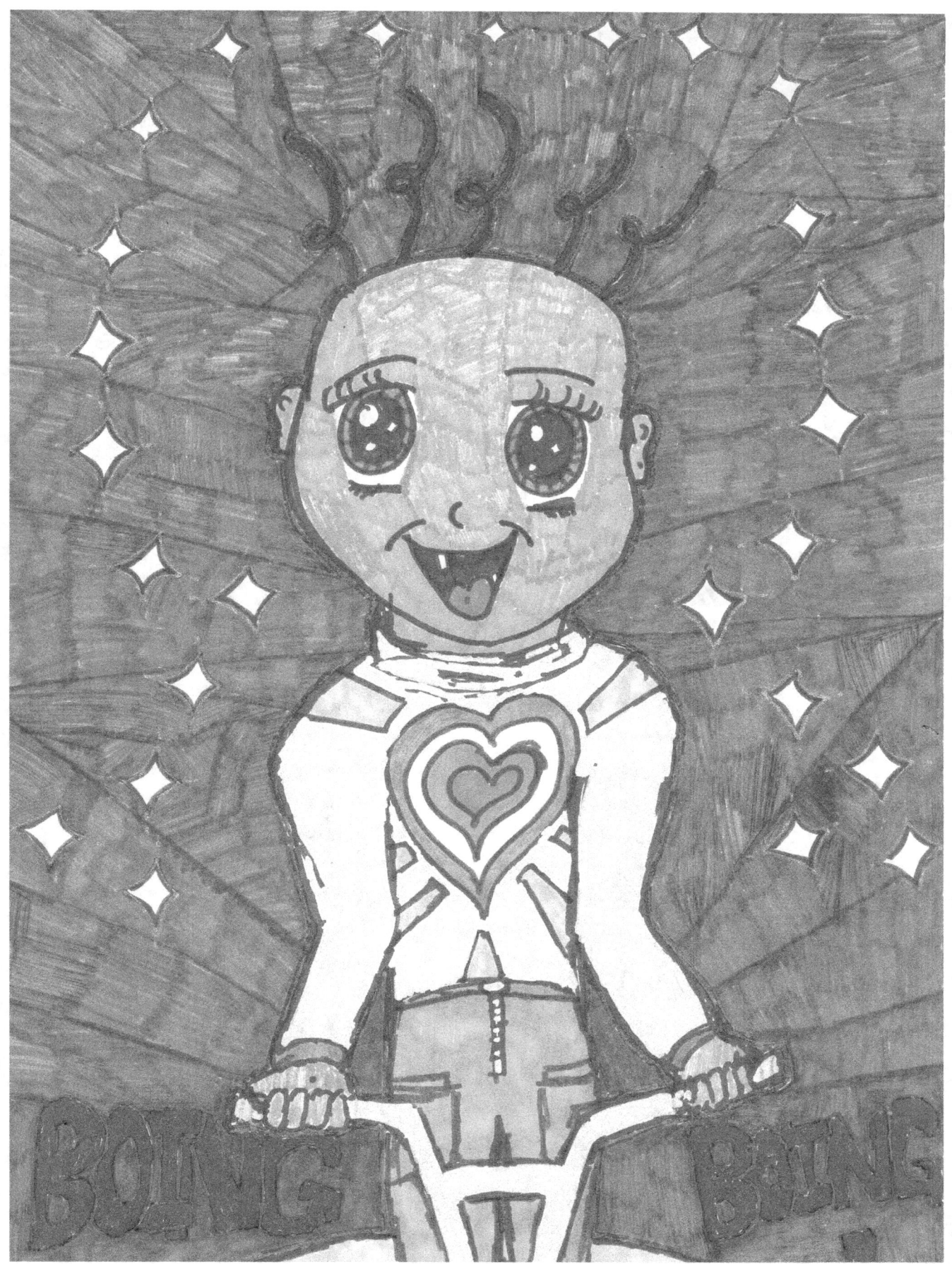

Recent Mixed Media Releases

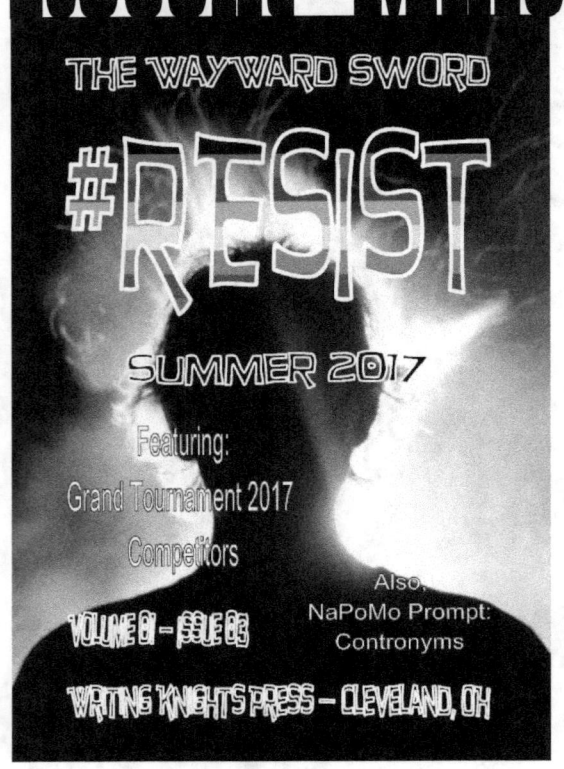
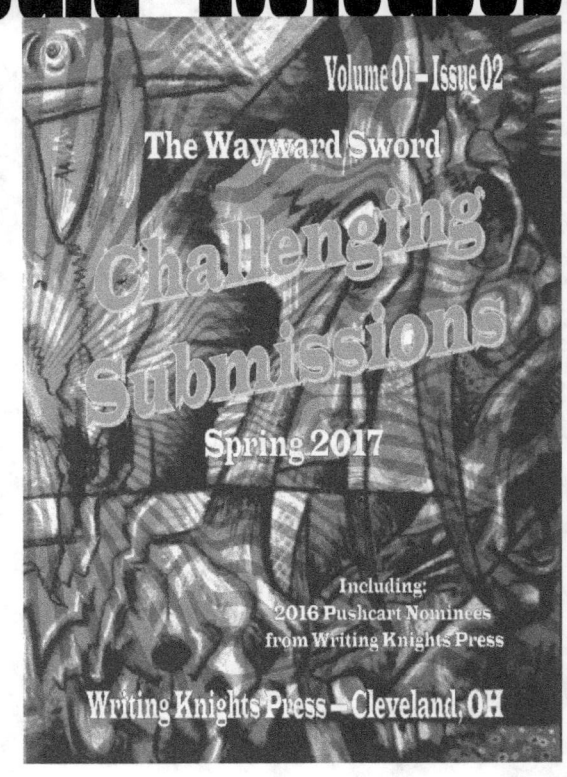
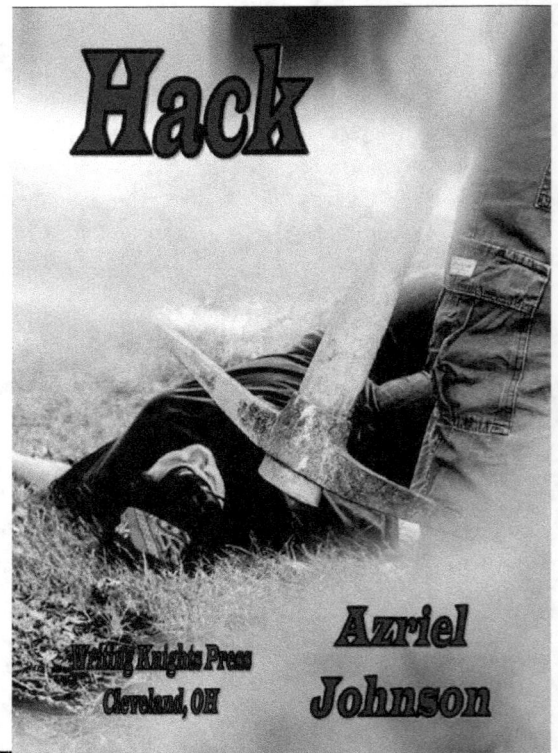

Find More Releases at WritingKnights.com

www.ingramcontent.com/pod-product-compliance
Lightning Source LLC
Chambersburg PA
CBHW062204220526
45470CB00009B/2910